Beyond the Rapids

HEATHER J. BENNETT

WESTBOW
PRESS®
A DIVISION OF THOMAS NELSON
& ZONDERVAN

WestBow Press books may be ordered through booksellers or by contacting:

WestBow Press
A Division of Thomas Nelson & Zondervan
1663 Liberty Drive
Bloomington, IN 47403
www.westbowpress.com
1 (866) 928-1240

Because of the dynamic nature of the Internet, any web addresses or links contained in this book may have changed since publication and may no longer be valid. The views expressed in this work are solely those of the author and do not necessarily reflect the views of the publisher, and the publisher hereby disclaims any responsibility for them.

Any people depicted in stock imagery provided by Getty Images are models, and such images are being used for illustrative purposes only.
Certain stock imagery © Getty Images.

Unless otherwise indicated, all scripture quotations are from The Holy Bible, English Standard Version® (ESV®). Copyright ©2001 by Crossway Bibles, a division of Good News Publishers. Used by permission. All rights reserved.

Scripture quotations marked (New American Standard Bible) taken from the New American Standard Bible® (NASB), Copyright © 1960, 1962, 1963, 1968, 1971, 1972, 1973, 1975, 1977, 1995 by The Lockman Foundation Used by permission. www.Lockman.org

ISBN: 978-1-9736-8947-8 (sc)
ISBN: 978-1-9736-8948-5 (e)

Library of Congress Control Number: 2020907248

Print information available on the last page.

WestBow Press rev. date: 07/07/2020

DEDICATION

This book is first and foremost dedicated to Jesus Christ. He loved us so much that He left His home and lived a life of hardship and suffering in human flesh. He took the penalty for our sin on the cross to reconcile those who believe in Him back to our heavenly Father. After He rose from the dead, He ascended to heaven and will soon come again. Glory be to His name on high!

This book is also in remembrance of my late husband and best friend, James Shannon Bennett. He taught me to live to the fullest, to be fearless, confident, and committed to what's most important.

ACKNOWLEDGEMENTS

I THANK OUR Lord Jesus Christ, for without Him, this book would have never taken shape. Jake and Lizzy, my two miracles, you are well beyond your years due to the many transitions you've faced. You've taught me far more about Jesus than you'll ever know and challenge me in my own walk with the Lord. I would also like to acknowledge my father and mother, Sam and Ida Jayne Hoye, who have loved me unconditionally and reflected different attributes of Jesus to me – my dad's faithful study of the Word and my mother's care for the poor, the lonely, and the hurting. They also provided significant contributions to this book with editing and direction. I'd also like to thank my sister, Tara Tharp, a talented writer and English teacher, for her editing contributions. I also want to thank Karen Hollenbeck who prayerfully edited this book, providing rich insights and detailed edits, journeying with me to the end as I discerned the final chapters. I thank Rebekah Blair from Sydney, Australia, a gifted artist who voluntarily painted the cover of this book, and became a part of our family's journey in Cambodia. Many thanks also for the contributions of my friends who voluntarily provided feedback in the initial rough drafts: Terese Luikens in Sandpoint, ID, who is on the journey to author her first book, Jean McAllister in Seattle who sojourned with me in Rwanda and is already a published author, and Jessica Brubaker who I also came to know on the football fields of Rwanda. I also thank the Sandpoint Christian Writer's Group, which helped me to refine my writing skills to use words on a page to point to the Author of the greatest story ever told – the gospel of Jesus Christ.

PREFACE

T HIS BOOK WAS bathed in tears, requiring lots of Kleenex as I pondered the memory boxes of life. I began writing this on the heels of my husband's death to record how we fell in love so that I would not forget. I wanted to pass something down to my children so that they, too, could remember their father, his character, and bits and pieces of his life story. I wanted them to know they were loved by their dad, and it was through our love that they were born. Most importantly, my desire and prayer was and is that Jake and Lizzy will know the richest treasure – that they are loved, cherished and adored by their Heavenly Father.

~ 1 ~

HIS TIMING

L IKE RAFTING A river, life doesn't go in a straight, even course. We aren't guaranteed a safe trip, where everything works out smoothly. We might even find ourselves outside the boat, holding onto the rope as we gasp for breath. Thus it is with my story and journey. I will begin with one of those intense rapids, where my life didn't go as planned, and I found myself gripping the rope tightly while the boat continued through the currents.

January 27, 2012 (Spokane, Washington)

Nurse Jane from Hospice comes to check on James. She always brings comfort along with her medical tools. I am eager to find answers and to understand how much time is left. After checking his vitals, she sits in the living room with my mom, Ida Jayne, and me as the sun drops behind the house on this short day of winter, where it is already dark by 4:30 p.m. After listening to us share the recent changes we have seen with James, Nurse Jane says gently, "I'm not always right, but I think he has a few days left."

The news isn't shocking. He has hardly been eating or drinking as we have been struggling to drop Ensure into his mouth by a straw. From all the materials and conversations, not eating and drinking is a clear sign of dying—or rather, going home.

I ask Nurse Jane about my daughter's birthday party, which is planned for the next day. We've already delayed it a week. "Could you host it at the church or somewhere else?" she suggests.

Lizzy, like any other seven-year old, has been talking about and anticipating this day for weeks...months. I am resistant to changing it, as I know moving the party will break her already fragile heart. She has wanted my undivided attention these last four months, but all my energy and time has been given to James. Our daily mother-daughter moments of drawing closer together, such as reading the Bible and praying each night, have been stripped away so many times in all the chaos. So I pray, *Lord, please allow James to make it through Lizzy's birthday.*

Yet I am full of heightened anticipation and nervousness. *What will I do if James dies during her birthday party?* This thought crosses my mind too many times, and I continue to fight it with faith that God will give him the time.

January 28, 2012 (Spokane, Washington)

Idjy, the name my mom chose when she became a grandmother, helps me decorate the house with Lizzy, using balloons, streamers, and a banner that says, "Happy Birthday!" Our little home is transformed into party central with pinks, purples, and pastels. I am amazed to see my mom stay so strong for Lizzy.

Two other women from my church small group, Mallory and Melissa, arrive to help us get ready for the party. Melissa has faithfully visited our home over the last few months, bringing her cute little dog and games. Tonight, she's arrived wearing her pajamas and smiles. She had the bright idea for Lizzy to have a pajama party rather than another Barbie party (for which I am grateful). Mallory arrives with a salon of at least twenty different shades of nail polish.

During the party, Idjy stays with James in the bedroom so that I can be a part of the celebration. Once, my mom calls me into the room, and several other times I catch moments to be with James, hold his hand, and shed tears. It is such a paradox to see the vibrancy of life in the next room while death is creeping in at our bedroom door.

My mom and I both tell James about the party. We hope he'll hold on to life for one more day, and we imagine that he might appreciate the sound of giggles from all the first-graders in the next room. "Hearing is one of the last things to go," my mom reminds me.

In spite of my mental exhaustion from entertaining people in our home and my nagging worry about him dying during the party, I feel an unexplainable peace. The Creator of all, *Elohim*, has sent Melissa, Mallory, and all these little girls into our home to comfort Lizzy and our family. They are bringing us *shalom* when everything else feels out of control.

Towards the end of the party, Lizzy asks me if her friends Celestine and Ella can come see her dad. I am hesitant because James has been on a constant dose of morphine, and the whites of his eyes are visible. I am worried about how this might impact these young girls.

I ask Lorri, Ella's mom, and she says, "Ella has been praying for James. I think it would be good for her."

Celistine, Ella, and Lizzy walk into our bedroom. Lizzy crawls up on her daddy's lap with a heart-shaped note that says, "I LOVE DAD", and I grab my camera and take what will be the last picture of James. It is a picture filled with sadness, joy, suffering, and triumph.

When everyone leaves, I am filled with gratitude for this answered prayer. This is one event under heaven that will surely be treasured in my heart forever.

January 29, 2012 (Spokane, Washington)

I hold his now limp hand—the right hand that has remained strong over the last four months. He looks like someone on a commercial for a humanitarian organization—malnourished, with a brittle and frail frame. Only bone and skin remain on his arms and legs, and his face is gaunt. Sitting by his hospital bed, safely at home, I lay my head on his chest, being careful not to touch the needle in his arm, which pumps morphine into his bloodstream.

His pale, almost blue body smells sweet from the vanilla body wash the Hospice nurse has used for his last bath. If he could talk, he'd be grumbling about this fragrance since he has always been a manly man. I chuckle. James loves to make me laugh. I miss his silly jokes and untimely remarks. Thinking about his humor now makes me start to cry. He hasn't been able to speak a word in weeks.

When his breathing stops, I count—one-one-thousand, two-one-thousand, three-one-thousand—and then sigh when he inhales once more. The Hospice literature and nurses have explained that this would happen in his last days. At least he is home—in bed, with his family around him.

Lifting my head and still holding his hand, I look at my wedding band. The silver is scratched and worn from nearly twelve years of marriage. I had thought we'd grow old together, that I would be holding his hand while sitting on the porch of a home where our children and grandchildren would come to celebrate our fiftieth wedding anniversary and other big milestones. But that picture of our future has been washed away with my tears.

Tick. Tock. Tick. Tock. How many hours, minutes, seconds remain? The time is so near. Our life together is being swallowed up by the ticking of a clock.

For the last four months, I have wanted James to speak about his desires for this little family of his, but our time has been short, and the disease has taken away our ability to have those conversations.

Yet I know that God's timing is perfect, for he is the Creator, the Potter, who appointed the seasons and time. Through the exhausting decisions and hardships of these past four months, he has been molding our family's hearts to be more like His.

For everything there is a season, and a time for every
matter under heaven:
a time to be born, and a time to die;
a time to plant and a time to pluck up what is planted.
–Ecclesiastes 3:1–2
New American Standard Bible

~ 2 ~

HIS PLANS

WHEN TAKING A boat downstream, we must know the season. Is it high water or low water? Is there turbulent weather in the forecast? All these factors can significantly alter the course to take downstream. After making these observations and determining the right approach, we push our boats out onto the river with confidence. However, inevitably the unexpected occurs—the paddlers don't paddle in rhythm or the storm comes sooner than anticipated. This leads us into unknown rapids, which we have to maneuver downstream. In the same way, I had mapped out a course for my life, but the unexpected occurred, leading me to people and places I had not dreamed and situations for which I was not prepared.

August 24, 1978—August 1997 (Chattanooga, Tennessee)

I was born with a full head of black hair and a tan skin tone, features I was told I inherited from the black Dutch. The rumor was we had an Indian princess in our line, but that may have been an old wives' tale.

Though Heather was a popular name in the 1970s, one of my great grandmothers never could get the name right. She kept saying, "Feather, Feather?" Interestingly "feather" stuck with me—not as a name, but as a part of my character. Like a bird on the edge of the nest, I was always seeking to explore. One time my parents lost me during bath time, and after frantically looking everywhere, they eventually found me in our yard, hanging from the limb on the tree with only half my pajamas on. I hadn't gone far, but I was looking to spread my wings and go further.

I was raised in the core of the Bible belt in the mid-sized city of Chattanooga, Tennessee. We moved to Signal Mountain when I was six years old because my parents wanted a small-town feel. They had both grown up in little towns. My dad, Samuel Aaron Hoye, grew up in Fayetteville, West Virginia, and my mom grew up in South Pittsburg, Tennessee.

Signal Mountain was a bit like *Mr. Roger's Neighborhood,* where people greet you when you pass by and bring pies to welcome new people in the community. It was so safe that our doors remained unlocked 24–7. We lived in a big house, although we always thought it was small compared to the mansions along the bluff. My dad worked at a large insurance company, and my mom was a high school English teacher. Both of them had to work full-time jobs to afford our lifestyle.

Faith was a part of life, and I really didn't know anything different. The majority of the people I knew were a part of a local church. I grew up at First Presbyterian Church in downtown Chattanooga, and we were there most every Sunday morning, Sunday evening, and Wednesday nights, too. As a little girl, I believed that Jesus saved me from my sins and often prayed for the smallest things, even kneeling by my bed when I lost my shoes. Nearly every time, God would show me that they were right up under my nose, hiding under the bed. Every time He answered, I would go from a state of worry to a state of peace. In these small moments I realized that Jesus cared for the small, practical details of my life.

In these small moments I realized that Jesus cared for the small, practical details of my life.

Attending church seemed stuffy and uncomfortable, dry and dull. I always had to look my finest, so getting ready for church was an ordeal— rolling up those itchy hose and wearing shiny shoes that made my feet hurt. *Phew!* I despised them, along with the flower-patterned dresses my mom and her lady friends loved. *Why couldn't I just wear pants and flip flops? Why did I have to be all dolled up?* I sometimes wished I could roll over and play sick.

I'd go to Sunday school and hear the stories of the Bible, and the teacher encouraged us to memorize Scripture. I didn't, though. My mom could barely get me to read books written for my age, so the Bible was daunting. After class, I'd walk to the fellowship hall to watch the live, televised sermon and would often fall asleep on my mother's shoulder. As soon as the service was over, I'd eagerly jump into line for a chilled bottle of Coca-Cola. I needed that bubbly carbonation to perk up after taking a nap.

After church we'd sometimes take a forty-five-minute drive to see my mother's family in South Pittsburg, which was one of my favorite places because everyone knew everybody, and every neighbor seemed to have some relation to my own family. Sometimes I was envious that my cousins lived so close to one another, while I lived what seemed to be so far away in Chattanooga.

My grandmother, Johnny Bell Hewgley (whom we called "Nony"), was a woman of class and dignity. She grew up during the Great Depression, and her family survived because of her dad's restaurant. I always noticed how she cleaned every Ziplock bag and let nothing go to waste. She made large quantities of food and then divvied it up into little reusable TV tray dinners to store in her big freezer. She had also endured the hardship of World War II. After being newly married, her husband Bill had gone off to war when she was pregnant with my mom.

Grandaddy Bill was kind and rooted for the underdog, but when he came back from the war, he was rough around the edges. My family told me that before the war he had been sensitive and caring, and Nony once said that he had never returned from the war emotionally. I only remember him sitting on the recliner, smoking cigarettes and wearing big overalls. He died of a heart attack before I stepped out of high school.

My fondest memories of my grandparents' old country house were watching the big, slimy bullfrogs gather under the porch light and capturing lightning bugs in glass jars before they flew off to the stars. Their hearth became a stage, and the house became a canvas that sparked my imagination.

Before my grandfather died, they bought a house in town. Our Sunday family gatherings continued in this new home even after his death. My uncles and aunts would bring a dish that usually included many casseroles—sweet potato, green bean, broccoli cheese, chicken, squash, or corn pudding. My grandmother made the most delicious homemade rolls from scratch, and there were always desserts. Every dish at the table was hand-painted by Nony, typically with roses like the ones she grew in her yard. We'd stack our plates full of food, and the adults would sit together in the dining room while all seven of us cousins would sit at the round table on the screened porch. There was always plenty of laughter around the table as we picked on one another and made light of every situation.

After the big feast, Nony's dining room became a great white tent filled with ladder-back chairs draped with sheets. We would always mess up her well-kept home, but after playing, everything had to go back to its proper place. If we whined, we'd be sent to the wooden pouting chair. She was strict, and she loved us dearly.

After cleaning up the dinner mess, we'd look through Nony's old photo albums. When we were older, we'd watch old VHS videos and reminisce about the crazy things we had done when we were younger. Over the years, we also enjoyed swimming in the creek, roller skating down sidewalks, or popping into one of our family's many homes around the corner (our extended family practically owned the entire block).

In spite of my traditional Southern upbringing, I often became friends with people who weren't from the South. Sarah entered my first-grade classroom wearing overalls, with her wavy brown hair puffed up in an afro. Sarah's family was Jewish, and through her friendship I learned about Hanukkah and Bat mitzvahs. Each year I got a little jealous around Christmas time, because Sarah would receive expensive gifts eight days in a row, but we only got one day of gifts with one big gift.

I loved going to her house to play with her Cabbage Patch dolls or hand-paint tiles to hang on their kitchen walls. Her mother was so artistic, and their house was full of creativity and color. Downstairs, they had a hot tub with a huge saltwater aquarium full of exotic fish, and they had Mario Brothers video games, something my sister and I weren't allowed to have. In my youthful eyes, their big, beautiful white-paneled home looked like a dollhouse.

Sarah and I remained close friends until she went into private school in seventh grade. The last time I saw her was at her Bat mitzvah, a grand occasion with ice sculptures, dancing and elegance that was held at the Chattanooga Choo Choo Hotel.

My friend Meghan and I spent most of our middle and high school years together, and we often found ourselves off the beaten path from our traditional Southern culture. We'd dance to African drums on the streets downtown during night fall concerts or sip lattés and eat European desserts in the art district over long conversations that went late into the night. Hitting the trails at Rainbow Lake or watching the sunset over the Tennessee River at Signal Point, we often dreamt about going to Africa. She wanted to be a primatologist like Jane Goodall or Dian Fossey, and I wanted to be a photographer for *National Geographic* or a visual anthropologist.

When I graduated from high school, my mom gave me the Dr. Seuss book *Oh, the Places You'll Go* and said, "The best things I can give you are wings." True to my great grandmother's misunderstanding of my name, I had grown feathers and was ready to spread my wings a bit further. I had my sights on the other end of the country, west of the Cascade Mountains, and was hoping to attend Evergreen State College, a non-traditional institution where students walked around in Birkenstocks, but in the end I accepted an invitation to Appalachian State University in Boone, North Carolina.

The day of my high school graduation, I had already packed my bags to move to the Ocoee River nearly fifty miles away, where I had found a job in a photo lab, printing pictures for rafting companies. I was hoping this job would take me one step closer to a future career as a photographer.

After walking the aisle along with other graduates from Hixson High School, I tossed my hat in the air and drove my black Jeep Wrangler with the top down, music blaring, my hair whipping in the warm summer air. As I drew closer to the Ocoee River, I felt free from the boundaries of being an adolescent.

While working at a local photo lab outsourced by the various rafting companies day after day, I watched the same machine spit out photos of people slapping their paddles together in a high-five, the guides catching air in the back, with everyone in the boat laughing as they rode through the rapids. Before long, I grew tired of smelling the fumes of the chemicals and transporting film to and from the photographer who was stationed at the Double Trouble rapid.

One day while sitting on the bank of the river, listening to the repetitive sounds of the crashing waves and the people cheering, I mustered the nerve to strike up a conversation with the photographer, who had brown hair with steaks of gray and an unshaven face. As I was only eighteen, I looked up to him as someone I'd want to emulate, and I shared my aspiration of becoming a professional photographer.

"You know, the Eagle Adventure Company is hiring," he told me.

After work that day, I took the plunge and called for an interview. Young and ambitious, I was delighted when the manager at the company offered me the job and a $1,400 salary for the entire summer.

The first day I arrived, I kicked up the dust along the rough and rugged Eagle Ranch Road in my Jeep and was met by a man wearing a frayed baseball cap, tan pants, and a black jacket, who greeted me with a grin and a handshake. I was immediately drawn to James and learned that he was the low and high ropes manager at the ranch.

As James helped me set up my tent, I was ecstatic to be trading my parents' three-bedroom brick and mortar house for a home in the great outdoors. I loved waking up at the crack of dawn, snuggled in my sleeping bag, and smelling the smoke from the previous night's fire. I enjoyed breaking out of the tent and heading down the trail to drink hot cocoa, eat a hot breakfast from the kitchen, and prepare with my coworkers for a long summer day on the river.

That first night, some of the river guides gathered around the campfire, and I sat next to James on one of the benches made by Claude, a true Copperhill local, who handled all the maintenance at the ranch. He reminded me of my grandfather, often wearing overalls, with what was left of his hair graying on top.

As James and I got to know one another, our conversation continued late into the night. James told me about the youth groups he led through trust falls and down the rappelling tower that he had helped build. He also told me about his favorite rock climbing spots and his adventures as a river rafting guide. Throughout the summer, we spent night after night by the fire pit, talking about our families, interests, and faith as the fire crackled and its glowing flames danced across our faces.

James grew up in the small town of Marks, Mississippi. At the age of five he was diagnosed with leukemia and was treated at the children's hospital in Memphis, which was about seventy miles away. He shared with me how two friends he had made during his treatments died. When he was eight years old, he was diagnosed with testicular cancer, but by the age of eighteen, he was completely cancer free.

Survival was James's motto—whether it was about surviving cancer or surviving in the outdoors by setting traps for squirrels, hunting with a bow and arrow, figuring out how to access water from a leaf when there was no other water source, or starting a fire with flint and steel or friction. He loved gear—guns, knives, machetes, compasses, backpacks, survival books, ropes—and aspired to live on his own in the woods like John "Grizzly" Adams, whom he grew up watching on television.

He showed me an article in the *Atlantic Journal* about his battle with cancer and how it had led to his new career in the outdoors. I treasured the article, which dubbed him "Indiana James," because it showed how he had overcome tragedy and testified to his strength, courage, and overall character, all things I was starting to adore about him.

I was amazed by his courage. I had never experienced great difficulty and wondered how I would've handled the fires of life he had endured. James was genuine and honest, sharing how he had misspent his high school days by drinking heavily. His choices had led to two DUIs, and because he didn't take high school seriously, he graduated with a GED. By the time he was twenty, he had become an addict, but when he was twenty-two, he stopped drinking cold turkey, left his retail job in Atlanta, and joined Eagle Adventure Company. Coming to the ranch marked a new start for his life.

James was raised in a Baptist church and attended youth group. We shared the same moral grounding and a similar faith, though neither of us was strong in obedience. We were both rebellious and often rationalized our sin, even though we knew deep down that certain choices were not in alignment with our faith. Similar to James, I often got drunk with friends and was addicted to cigarettes. But as I spent more time with him, I began drinking soda instead of beer and resisting the peer pressures around us. River guides love to party, and it was refreshing for me not to try to fit in to that scene.

On our day off each week, we started spending time together, sometimes traveling to Atlanta, where James would hunt through bins of discounted army and survival gear at Brigade Quartermaster. Though I didn't care about that store, I wanted to be with him.

We also started to have unofficial dates at the local laundromat, where James always tried to make me laugh by adorning my head with underwear as people passed by the glass window. I always gave him a little punch in the arm for that.

I loved catching glimpses of him as he guided rafts through the Broken Nose and Double Trouble rapids, where I was stationed to take pictures. At first, he greeted me from afar with a wave. Over time, he started to blow kisses that I caught like butterflies.

When we were back at the ranch, he came down off the rappelling tower Aussie-style, zipping down on the rope face-forward like Peter Pan, and then planted a kiss on my lips. Anyone standing nearby erupted in cheers. As James wooed my heart that summer, I began to fall in love.

So at the end of that summer, I thought we'd be together forever, but he broke up with me on our last night before I headed off to Boone. Because he was six years older than me, he thought it would be better for me to begin at Appalachian State with a fresh start. But I was devastated and angry. How could he seem to love me and then throw me away? For the next several months, I wished I'd never even met him. My plans had been disrupted, as I never planned to fall in love. I came to the ranch full of excitement, but I left the ranch with a shattered heart and demolished dreams.

We make our own plans, but the LORD decides where we will go.
-Proverbs 16:9
New American Standard Bible

~ 3 ~

HIS STRENGTH

THE VERY SOUND of the rapids exudes power, reminding us how little we are in comparison. They can turn over boats, wipe out homes, and humble prideful men. They have a way of showing who is weak and who is strong. I was fully aware of this power while also fully aware of my weaknesses every time I paddled. The more I jumped into the river, the more I understood that my weaknesses were actually the way to great strength.

August 1997–August 1998 (Boone, North Carolina)

My new roommate at Boone was Jaime Matthews. She had blond hair, blue eyes and wore a T-shirt with long athletic shorts. The moment we met, she was convinced I was a foreigner. As we started talking about setting up our room, I mentioned that I didn't think we needed a television. Her jaw dropped to the floor, and she was bound to change my "foreign" perceptions. Though I grew up watching a lot of television, after living at the rustic outdoor ranch, I found joy in not having one.

On top of the television shock, our dorm was mostly filled with students in the Watauga program, an alternative to the core curriculum. Since I couldn't go to Evergreen State College, this was my best shot. We still don't know why she was assigned to live with our program, but she became one of my best friends.

While I carried a camera, she carried a basketball, and for awhile we both wondered if we'd ever find anything in common. But before the semester was rolling, I was addicted to Jaime's teeny bopper television shows. We also discovered we both had torn ACLs and that we both enjoyed skiing. As we got to know one another, she began to hear a lot about James. She had to endure my sorrows as I talked with him on the phone and pleaded for us to be together. When El Nino hit the coast of North Carolina, it seemed to mirror the internal storm in me. I felt myself sinking into a deep depression.

Then one day, James agreed to move to Banner Elk, which was a five-minute drive from Boone, where he found a job at the ski shop at Ski Beech.

I checked out of the college life of football games, parties with beer, and sororities, and spent every weekend and every possible moment with James. Jaime and James became good friends, often ganging up to tease me like two older siblings. James helped Jaime and me get part-time jobs at Ski Beech, where we stocked shelves and worked the cash registers together every weekend. The job offered us free ski passes and cash for books, gasoline and food. For James, the job paid him just enough to afford an apartment, feed his old Bronco, and live on Tony's frozen pizza or whatever he could scramble up. Cooking was not his forte. Rather than stashing any extra from his paychecks into stocks, bonds and mutual funds, he invested in gear: snowboard, helmet, beanie hats, gloves, the finest ski pants and jackets. From head to toe, he was outfitted in black, which suited what the shop called "mud skiing," for when temperatures rose above freezing, skiers and boarders found themselves sliding over mud puddles as the snow and ice melted away. James eagerly took in every opportunity to engage in this uniquely Southern sport, while Jaime and I usually opted to stay and work longer hours in the store.

One night while we were working, James came in covered in mud, grass stains, and grinning from ear to ear. No matter what the conditions, he was bound and determined to learn the art of snowboarding (or mud-boarding) on his own. No matter how many falls he took or how much pain he experienced, he enjoyed every moment—and, like anything else, it didn't take him long to master it.

After the ski season ended in March, James packed his car to return to Eagle Adventure Company, and I was right behind him, driving five-hours through the lush green Appalachian Mountains to the Blue Ridge

Mountains of Tennessee every weekend to work at the ranch, where I began training as a river guide.

James saw something in me that I couldn't see—an untapped confidence and desire for more than the lens I carried. He helped me harness the courage to go after the full life I longed for on the other side of the camera. He encouraged me to grab a paddle, jump in the back seat of the raft, and live a little, saying, "You can do it." He told me that women are much better guides than men, because women don't rely on their muscles but use the power of the water.

James and other experienced guides took us rookies down the Ocoee River each day, teaching us how to guide. I picked up a whole new vocabulary—*eddy, hydraulics, reading water, thwarts* and *sweet spots.* I learned how to use my guide belt in emergencies and how to throw a rope to someone who'd fallen into the water, which is much harder than it sounds in a fast current. I learned to watch the patterns of the water to guide the boat from one point to another.

I also learned to get tough as we picked up the rafts and loaded them on the trailer, squatting low to use my legs rather than my back, raising it to my chest, then shifting it above my head, where I held it steady and then stacked it on top of the other rafts. Then we unloaded the rafts and walked them above our heads from the parking lot and down to the river. I tried my best to keep the boats steady as my muscles shook, though I often wanted to quit and ask for a break from the men who were working with me. But I kept my mouth shut and kept going. *Tough it out, girl,* I would say to myself. When I heard the sound of the water crashing over the dam onto the rocks below and saw the class IV rapid of the lower Ocoee, my heart pounded and my stomach curled. Like *The Little Engine That Could,* I repeated in my mind, *I think I can, I think I can, I think I can.*

Training in the cold and rain was brutal, as even my splash jacket, gloves, wool socks and fleece were not enough to keep me from shivering. I always hoped a rookie wouldn't be put in the guide's seat on those days, because there was a higher potential that I would have to swim.

On the days I was chosen to guide, I'd place the boat in the river by Grumpy's Rapid, and the chill of the icy waters would shoot up my spine, intensifying my edginess. While all the rookies sat patiently on the thwart of the raft with their paddles resting on their laps, I'd stand nervously holding the boat, afraid of making a wrong technical move that would send them to White Face, a rock that rafts wrapped around like a burrito before sinking, sending paddlers downstream towards the nasty hydraulic. Entering a hydraulic is like jumping into a massive washing machine, spinning around, then being shot out like a canon into whitewater, where you have to swim through a strong and choppy current, ingesting water as you gasp for air.

The entrance into Grumpy's Rapid was a mind game that often scrambled my thoughts, but I learned to ease the boat into the water and aim it upstream to ensure that we'd cross the rapid and hit the sweet spot. Then I'd push the boat, jump in the back, and yell, "ALL FORWARD!" Reaching my paddle far out and perpendicular with the boat, I'd use the force of the water to keep the boat angled upstream. "DIG! DIG! DIG!" I'd yell. A sense of relief always washed over me as we entered the sweet spot, and then rode the current downstream, passing White Face and the keeper hydraulic on our right.

Whenever I'd catch a glimpse of James standing on the rocky shores catching safety with a rope bag in his hands, ready to rescue us if the raft flipped and we ended up in the water, I felt secure no matter how much I was falling apart inside. He'd put his thumb up with a nod and grin as if to say, "That's my girl." With him standing by and watching, I felt peace every time I entered the river.

Once when James was the trip leader, a customer fell out of the raft at Grumpy's Rapid and was carried into the keeper hydraulic. When James saw the man go towards the hydraulic, he swam hard, rescued the man, and hauled him to shore. Though the man didn't break any bones, the hydraulic sucked his pants right off, along with his wallet and keys! (Special tip: when river rafting, wear a wet suit or shorts with a *tight* waistband). James's experience with illness gave him both empathy and compassion, and so he was not only able to doctor the man's wounded bottom, but also to care for his wounded pride.

As part of river guiding 101, we learned to swim class III and IV whitewater rapids and how to curl in a ball if we were caught in a hydraulic. For fun, we'd often jump into a small hydraulic to feel the sensation of swirling and being spit out. We also learned how to flip rafts over while swimming down the current and how to pull rafts off rocks.

Even after the intense training that spring, I never felt fully confident to guide customers down the river, but James was fully confident in me. Always cheering me on, he said it was time for a checkout trip since the summer season was upon us and guides were in high demand.

I dreaded the checkout trip, but when the day arrived, I was assigned a group of women from the local high school basketball team. As athletes, they were lightweight and would be able to paddle hard, but I was still nervous and nauseous. But James was near, setting safety downstream, and the trip began with success at Grumpy's Rapid.

I had never had trouble at the next rapid, Broken Nose, which is not nearly as technical, but I entered with a bad angle. Before I could yell a command, our noses were literally planted on a huge boulder in the middle of the river, and several girls were sucked out of the raft and into the choppy waters. As our boat started to sink, two girls climbed on top of the boulder, and I took off my guide belt and hooked the carabiner to the raft and began pulling against the relentless current. It felt like I was trying to pull a dump truck out of floodwaters. Then I saw James swimming across the rapid to save the day. He climbed aboard, tugged at the right spot, and the boat popped off the rock. Though hardly a flawless checkout trip, I was approved as a river guide.

As I continued to guide over the summer, I became more and more confident and learned to rely on the power of the water, as James had taught me, rather than my own strength. I endured more swims and was trapped under the raft after going through Hell's Hole Rapid, but every failure was a lesson learned with only a few cuts or bruises.

> *I learned to rely on the power of the water, as James had taught me, rather than my own strength.*

One day, we rode the Upper Ocoee, where the riverbed had been rerouted to create the 1996 Olympic Whitewater Course. The five-mile narrow course was intense, with back-to-back class V rapids that we had to learn to navigate with customers after only a few runs. Every time I went over the edge of the first rapid, which was like passing over a narrow waterfall as tall as our raft, I would clench hold of the back of the raft. Eventually I got the hang of it, and we were doing three to four trips a day.

Sometimes we took customers down more mild rivers, such as the Nantahala in North Carolina, but most of the guys, including James, were always looking for the big thrills. Once James convinced a group of guides to raft down the class VI Gauley River in West Virginia for a fun run since Lee, one of our Eagle guides, had been trained for it.

When we arrived at the river in the morning, I saw the dam where water was gushing with force like a massive fire hose. The river was wide when compared to the Ocoee, and I didn't know what to expect. My dad had grown up nearby and remembers being warned to stay away from the river because falling into it would "kill you." Looking at it, I had this same trepidation.

Halfway into the trip, James said he wanted to guide. While I had always looked up to him as one of the best guides, I was nervous since he'd never rafted the Gauley before. Lee explained what he needed to look out for while the rest of us sat on the shore to take a break.

When we got back in the boat to launch, we saw a massive rock wall at the entrance to a canyon where there seemed to be no escape. As we went through the intense rapids, we headed straight towards the rock wall and then hit it with force. To my surprise, we didn't turn over or get sucked into the churning waves, but bounced off, spun around and kept going down the river.

As I reflected on this time in my life much later, I thought of Psalm 18:2: "The Lord is my rock and my fortress and my deliverer, my God, my rock, in whom I take refuge, my shield, and the horn of my salvation, my stronghold." But at that moment, I was just thankful to be alive.

As I continued to improve my river guiding skills, I eventually became a team leader and caught safety and helped keep our team of boats together. Our company had very few female guides, but James was quick to give us a step-up, because he saw a maturity and humility in us that the other male guides couldn't see.

Everyday was an incredible adventure, filled with stories to retell as we gathered at our favorite Mexican restaurant after a fourteen-hour day in the scorching sun or pouring rain. I was living like I had never lived before. James had helped me conquer my fear of the rapids by trusting in the power of the water rather than my own strength. I felt assured by James's presence as he held my hand through the rapids of life and taught me to be strong, secure and confident. I didn't understand yet that my true strength and confidence needed to come from the Lord.

But he said to me, "My grace is sufficient for you, for my power is made perfect in weakness." Therefore I will boast all the more gladly of my weaknesses, so that the power of Christ may rest upon me. For the sake of Christ, then, I am content with weaknesses, insults, hardships, persecutions, and calamities. For when I am weak, then I am strong.
—2 Corinthians 12:9–10
New American Standard Bible

~ 4 ~

His Pursuit

J AMES AND I continued our life together. I still had to complete college but doing so seemed like an inconvenience. The only future I could see was being by James's side. In my impatience, I took eighteen-hour class loads so I could graduate as quickly as possible. But as I struggled to finish school in three and a half years, it seemed the tests I crammed for were mirroring some bigger tests on the horizon in the rapids of life.

1999–2000 (Boone, North Carolina)

As I continued on the fast track through college, James lived and worked in Banner Elk each winter, and Jaime, James and I continued to work at the retail store at Ski Beech. Every spring and fall, I'd make the commute each weekend to work at Eagle Adventure. It was tiring, but worth it to be with James.

Caught up in school, work, travel, and James, faith took a back seat. I didn't think I needed church, and so I went without it. I thought James was enough.

In the very liberal program at Watauga College, we had ethical and religious discussions in our history and English classes. When I read a biography about the Baptist preacher and activist Martin Luther King Jr., I really tripped over his adulterous affair—a detail that made me question the authenticity of his faith while ignoring my own hypocrisy. Surrounded by highly academic students who loved philosophy, poetry, and debating various world views, some students were like ravaging wolves when it came to Christianity. One Christian girl even left the program because she couldn't take all the darts being thrown at her beliefs. I admired her conviction, though, which I didn't have during that season of my life.

As I listened to the various arguments, blood rose in my face whenever peers refuted my faith, but I didn't join the debate. I hadn't even read the entire Bible, let alone all the books they had read, and so I felt I couldn't stand firm against their intellectual reasoning. I also knew I wasn't being obedient to God in some areas, and so I felt ashamed to say anything at all.

I also had more mainstream classes at Appalachian State that made me wrestle with my beliefs. In an ethics class, a discussion of euthanasia forced me to contemplate life and death. *If I were to care for someone who was suffering deeply, would I assist him with medication to speed up the process of dying? Would I want someone to live in a dormant state, hooked up to a machine, for days, months or years?* These questions caused me to evaluate my convictions about what was right and wrong. But rather than coming to any final conclusions, I hoped those decisions would not cross my path.

As I got further into my recreation management program, the classes became less abstract as I learned how to manage a campground or national park. Recreation was far less scholarly, and it also kept my mind on James, as I envisioned us owning a camp or running a rafting company together.

Then one day my mom phoned to tell me that my beloved grandmother, Nony, was dying in the hospital. "Do you want to come see her?" my mom asked.

My family and I had just spent Christmas with her. She had met James and told my parents that she had never seen two people sit so close to one another on the couch. She believed we would marry.

Though I loved Nony dearly, I rationalized that I didn't want to remember her sick in a hospital bed, but healthy and alive, as I'd last seen her. I couldn't bear to see her weak and frail, and so I decided to stay in Boone.

Nony died not soon after that phone call, and James and I attended her funeral together. She left behind a plan for handling her estate, with careful instructions about how to share the pieces from her home. She instructed all her children and grandchildren to draw numbers and then go around the table to select items in a nice and orderly fashion. Though it was a gift to sit with the family around her wooden table, going through her treasures from years of travel and her long history of hard living, her death was a heavy wake-up call. I felt young and invincible, healthy and alive. I didn't want to think about death, which was so final and unforgiving.

But later that year, on April 20, 1999, I turned on the television after classes and saw the nightmarish images of students running out of Columbine High School in complete disarray, trying to escape all the shooting. Sitting on the edge of the couch, I bowed my head in my hands and sobbed, *Why? What has gone wrong? Where is this world going?* Later, I learned that two students had taken the lives of thirteen people and then killed themselves. Then I heard the story about Rachel Scott, one of the victims. The gunman grabbed her hair and asked if she still believed in the Lord. She said, "You know I do." Then he said, "Well, go be with Him," and shot her in the temple.

Nony's death and the multiple deaths in Colorado stirred my heart to return to God, but I continued to feel that the only real and tangible thing in my life was James. But my time at college was nearing its end, and I still had no wedding ring on my finger, and so I started to wonder where James and I were going. While I loved being a river guide and working at the ski resort, I wanted to move to new, unexplored territory in the West. James, on the other hand, was in a sweet spot as the river manager at Eagle Adventure. He was perfectly content to stay in Tennessee, where he was thriving and respected.

During this climatic time, I was offered an internship at Keystone Resort in the Rocky Mountains of Colorado. I stubbornly decided to accept the internship telling James I'd go with or without him. When he decided to choose to come with me, our commitment became solidified.

One weekend my parents came to visit me, and we all met up to go for a nice dinner in a rustic restaurant in Banner Elk. Sitting in the candlelit room, James couldn't stop admiring the atmosphere. After a delicious meal and great conversation, James made a bold move. Looking at my parents, he said, "Will you allow me to take your daughter's hand in marriage?" Neither of my parents responded verbally, but their tears said it all. Without a ring or a proposal to me, James did what any Southern-raised gentleman would do: he asked for permission. He already knew my answer was "yes." I didn't care about wedding rings and proposals. He was all I wanted.

Not too long after, I was packing my bags for the Rocky Mountains. While I started my hospitality internship at Keystone, James found a job working in Buena Vista, Colorado as a river guide on the Arkansas River with a company that had led groups on overnight trips and was situated in a landscape unlike any place in the Southeast. He seemed happy with his new adventures in the West, as there were so many new sports to try, higher mountains to climb and more extreme survival situations in the rugged terrain of Colorado.

On October 14, 2000, during my last semester of college, when I was only twenty-two years old, I married James in a small church close to my grandmother's old house in South Pittsburg. We covered the sanctuary and fellowship hall in colorful fall leaves and filled it with candlelight, and every handmade invitation had a stamped fall leaf upon it. In reflecting on this image later, the fallen leaves seemed to foreshadow the season to come.

James returned to Colorado right after we married, but before I could pack my bags to join him, I had to graduate. So with my silver wedding band on my left hand, I stayed in Boone to finish my final semester.

Two weeks after our wedding, as I was walking across campus to class, James phoned and somberly told me that his only brother, Brandon, who was my age, had shot himself.

Only two weeks before, Brandon had been lifting James up with all the other bachelors. He had sat at our reception table and stood beside us at our wedding. In the three years I dated James, I had never really had the chance to get to know him. James and I had been so wrapped up in each other.

As I packed funeral clothes for the trip to Yazoo City, Mississippi, I realized that I was embarking on the hardest journey I'd ever had to take. I still felt like an outsider in this new family, as I had only just met some of James's relatives at the wedding. When I arrived, my mother-in-law, Anita, was sitting at the dining room table, weeping, surrounded by family members and the pale faces of strangers. As I stood there trying to determine who was who and how they related to each other, I felt as if I was trying to pick up a thousand-pieced jigsaw puzzle after a tornado. Family members expressed regret that we had just shared a joyous occasion and now were gathering for a grievous reunion. I didn't know how to mourn and felt hollow and shallow. I worried that if I hadn't met James or lured him off to Colorado, he might have noticed that his brother was drowning in addiction, depression and despair. I had always wanted a brother, and I'd had a brother-in-law for two weeks, but now he was gone.

Before the funeral, James went into a private room at the funeral hall with his family, where Brandon's body lay in a casket. I wasn't invited because I wasn't part of the inner circle of this family. When the two large wooden doors closed, I heard James weep for the first time, a deep wail from a place I hadn't even known existed within him. I had never felt so distant from him, and I suddenly realized how little I knew about him, how little we had discussed his brother and his problems.

That night, James barely spoke as we lay on our backs on Brandon's twin bed, looking up at the ceiling. We didn't see the bloodstains that had been there days before, as someone had kindly repaired the wall and put on a fresh coat of paint.

The television on the wooden chest was on, and as I lay there listening, I heard the familiar voice of Ben Haden, the lead pastor of First Presbyterian Church, which I had attended as a child. As he spoke about forgiveness, God had my undivided attention. I knew that I needed to think about my own salvation and how I would stand before God on the day of my death, but I was in shock, and so I just listened rather than making any decisions. But I sensed that God was trying to speak to me and was inviting me to pursue Him rather than focusing all my attention on James. Later, I came across a passage in the book of James that reminded me of this defining moment in my life and marriage: "Draw near to God, and he will draw near to you. Cleanse your hands, you sinners, and purify your hearts, you double-minded. Be wretched and mourn and weep. Let your laughter be turned to mourning and your joy to gloom" (James 4:8–9).

I sensed that God was. . . inviting me to pursue Him rather than focusing all my attention on James.

We stayed with my in-laws at a house by a river for a few days, and as we ate catfish at a local restaurant, I scrutinized every word I said and every move I made. I was young, newly wed and felt completely alone and lost. I felt that if I made one small mistake, the pipes holding back the flood of grief would explode, and our house would flood again. I had never experienced a catastrophe before. James and his parents had been through years of battling cancer and won—twice! I was not prepared spiritually or emotionally to help them cope, and so I stood on the sidelines, feeling that there was nothing I could say or do. I knew that I wanted to draw near to God, but I didn't know how.

Despite this dark and yet divine interlude, the currents continued. Life went on. James returned to Colorado, and I went back to North Carolina. After two long months, I finally graduated in December 2000 and was shocked to be ranked in the top two graduates of our department.

My most difficult farewell was to Jaime, who had been such a good friend. I wished I could pack her up and take her along to Colorado, but I knew that our story of sharing so much life together was at its final page.

Like a pioneer, I left the South with my hopes set on a bright future with the one I loved, but tucked away in the closets of my soul were boxes of unanswered questions. Though James had pursued me by following me to Boone and then to Colorado and by asking my parents if he could marry me, I knew that God was also pursuing me, beckoning me to repent, but I had buried his invitation in a drawer.

"What do you think? If a man has a hundred sheep, and one of them has gone astray, does he not leave the ninety-nine on the mountains and go and search for the one that is straying?"
—Matthew 18:12
New American Standard Version

~ 5 ~

HIS DESIRE

SOMETIMES THERE ARE stretches of calm floating on the river, when you can put your paddles down to take in a sunset or listen to the music of the boat moving through the water. During these calm stretches, you can be present and enjoy the scenery with those in your boat. Shortly after I graduated from college, James and I entered such a season as newlyweds, getting to know more about each other in a new place.

2001–2002 (Summit County, Colorado)

Driving across the country, I passed by the gateway arch of St. Louis and through Kansas, with its rows of endless sunflowers, and then began climbing the rugged Rocky Mountains, traveling more than 1,350 miles to reach James and our new abode.

Our new home in Summit County was majestic and picturesque, so it is no wonder that people travel from all around the world to live there. Its pine trees and mountains are covered in snow most of the year. The landscape glows with yellow leaves from the aspen trees in autumn and is sprinkled with brilliantly colored wildflowers in the late spring. Our condo in Wilderness was a short drive from Breckenridge, Keystone, and many other ski resorts and popular hiking trails, such as Buffalo Mountain at 12,777 feet. The biking paths stretched along the Blue River and meandered through the vast playground right outside our back door. Nearly every day, we woke up to fresh powder and blue skies. With such towering peaks and massive canyons, I felt so tiny as I absorbed the enormity of our new homeland.

Fresh out of college, I looked and looked for a job. James helped me yet again, and I began working alongside him at another outdoor clothing shop while searching for a full-time job in recreational management. I enjoyed working in the shop with James and gained a nice wardrobe with all the pro-rates and freebies, but I was elated when I received a position at the Marriott Mountain Valley Lodge at Breckenridge Resort. I was offered a good starter salary, great benefits and the opportunity to have one foot indoors and the other outside. I enjoyed taking people hiking, snowshoeing, skiing and planning après ski parties and ice cream socials, but I had not yet learned how to manage people. So I had to step out of my comfort zone as I embarked on the new journey of working as a young professional. James was a natural with people, and so he cheered me on and gave me excellent advice.

We also continued to guide on the Arkansas River that summer as well as the Colorado River, where James got into river boarding. Before I knew it, he wanted to go face-level through a canyon of back-to-back rapids. I was hesitant, but I ended up loving it. I'd kick hard with my fins to sneak around the big rapids, but James always went straight for the middle, nose first. At the end of the day, as we floated along the river, we'd hold hands as we watched the sun set. The light cast a brilliant orange and pink glow on the mountains around us and made the river shimmer like gold.

Eventually my river guiding days came to an end due the workload at my job, but I was glad James had the outlet to continue guiding, as it was a natural fit. I had my own adventures in my job, getting to ride horses, participate in wild-west cattle drives, and eat at fine restaurants that were only accessible by gondola. I continued to guide people outdoors. On one youth hike, we saw a bear up-close in spring, which then followed us up the trail, but eventually departed. James and I were both getting the full Colorado experiences of our dreams.

James figured out how to ice climb, picked up the gear through his job, and then taught me. We had "dates" at frozen waterfalls. I loved chopping at the ice with the axe and kicking my foot for a good grip.

On the slopes, James picked up skiing and continued to snowboard, quickly advancing to racing down black diamonds at lightning speed. I tried to teach myself tele-mark skiing, but could never master it, so I trailed behind James on the blue runs, not feeling daring enough for the blacks. Since we didn't sync on the slopes, we would meet each other at the lift and ride up together.

James's desire to be outdoors and his love for the wilderness led him to join the Summit County Search and Rescue team, which was comprised predominantly of men who had the same excitement as James for life on the edge. Over time, the search and rescue team consumed his life outside work, as he'd be called out on all-night rescues for a skier who went out of bounds or snowmobile drivers who had driven off cliffs in the fog of the night.

As much as James and I were enjoying our "honeymoon" in the paradise of Colorado together, the tradeoff was becoming costly. To pay the bills, buy gas, groceries (with milk costing as much as $4), and cover our $800 rent for a studio apartment, we began to feel the pressure to make more money, work more hours and push harder. James, especially, was always trying to find a better career to fulfill his role as the "man" of the house. He found a job as a security officer at Keystone, which required him to work nights and weekends. He would come home worn out from dealing with people who were partying past hours in the hot tubs or pushing drink machines over balconies, though he loved keeping people in line and encouraging them to make better choices. He had always wanted to be a cop, but hadn't been able to due to his misspent youth. With our misaligned job schedules and his continued volunteer work with the Summit County Search and Rescue, we were being pulled apart. We no longer had the time or energy to go backcountry skiing in Mayflower Gulch or climb the soaring peaks around us. With that came arguments and a rift formed between us.

Towards the end of our first year of marriage, as I was putting on my vest for work on September 11, 2001, I saw an explosion on the television screen as a commercial plane crashed into one World Trade tower and then another. *More death. More suicide.* God had my undivided attention. Like most Americans, I was perplexed and mourning with those who had lost family and friends. However, as months went by, my selfish consumptions quickly overrode those nagging questions about life and death. Once again, I tucked them away.

James and I continued trying to build our careers and make some wise choices for the future. We found a 700-square-foot, two-bedroom condo up the road at Treehouse that was within our tight budget. The low cost meant a serious makeover was due. The beamed ceilings and kitchen cabinets were all painted black, and there was only a glass sliding door in the main room, with no windows, making the place extremely dark. But we took it.

My dad offered to come from Tennessee to help us fix it up, making the long journey and then spending most of his time with a paintbrush rather than a set of skis. It took three coats of paint to cover the black, from the inside of the cabinets to the ceiling. We also tore down the dark paneling that covered Sheetrock as we tried to give our new home a radical face-lift.

But with all the work, something wasn't right—not with the interior of the condo, but with my own interior. I had married the man I loved, had been swept away to a happily ever after, and was making a new dwelling with him in the most beautiful part of the country, but I felt miserable and lonely. No matter how much paint I had used to cover up my despair, it was still there. I could still see the black spots coming through all my desperate attempts to touch it up.

We had more and more disagreements, and when they got intensely emotional, James would say, "Heather, why don't we just get a divorce?" This word felt like a bullet to my heart. I'd say that I wasn't going to quit but typically ended up in a ball, crying in my pillow. James had always wanted to live alone in the woods, to live an adventurous life like the young man in *Into the Wild*, and so I started to believe that he regretted marrying me. I'd fallen in love with James, but now he wanted to walk away, to throw in his cards and leave me. This feeling of rejection was intensely painful. He never said he wanted to leave the search and rescue team or his job. I felt like he was choosing them over me.

When these hard times came, it felt like my "happily ever after" was like a dandelion seed being blown away. I realized the gravity of the word "commitment" through trial. Though I was only in my early twenties, I went into a mid-life crisis, wondering what my purpose was and why I had been placed on this planet. I wanted to escape the pain of my marriage and find a way to fill the deep and wide hole in my heart. I had abandoned

Jesus and was trying to fill my heart with James' love instead, but I didn't realize that my deepest need for love could never be satisfied in James.

Around this time, as I was meandering though the local Wal-Mart, I saw the book *The Purpose Driven Life* by Rick Warren. Drawn to the word "purpose," I picked up a copy and then read and reread each chapter. Each page convicted me, and I recognized my need for fellowship in a church. I agonized over this conviction, because I loathed wearing dresses and looking my Sunday best. I felt like I had to appear my best on the outside, because I knew that internally I was wreck.

Not too far from where we lived, I stumbled upon a little nondenominational congregation called Dillon Community Church. James and I went together the first Sunday. Wearing blue jeans and a mountain beard, Pastor Brian Post preached with a conviction and passion that I had never heard before. I was intrigued, and it felt like I had been given new ears and a softer heart to receive his teaching. But James was skeptical, because they showed a clip from the movie *Peter Pan* to illustrate a point, which he felt was inappropriate.

But I managed to convince James to give the church another try, and so Sunday after Sunday, as our work schedules allowed, we began attending the church. I often went alone and was moved at every sermon. I began sitting in the front row, taking notes on the incredible messages flowing from the pulpit and how God was speaking to me from His word. When they announced that a women's Bible study on the book of Jonah was about to begin, I felt drawn to sign up and arranged my work schedule so that I could attend the class each Thursday morning.

Though I was familiar with the story about the man caught in the big fish from my childhood, it became a vivid Picasso painting as we observed it with a magnifying glass and discovered many hidden treasures. Pastor Brian led the class, and his gift for explaining the Scriptures and pulling out the cultural and historical background gave us rich understanding of the context. I began devouring the word of God and couldn't get enough to satisfy my appetite—like eating a delicious home-cooked meal and then needing to go for another helping. But unlike food, the more I devoured, the more I hungered—and I never got a bellyache from consuming too much of God's Word! I began reading through the Bible for the first time. Though it was difficult to understand, I realized it was possible to study on my own.

After Pastor Brian's teaching, we divided up into smaller groups. An older woman named Alice was my small group leader. She had short, curly gray hair, a petite figure, wore Southwestern jewelry, and had a gentle and quiet demeanor. Sitting still with her light pink Bible in her lap, she'd begin her questions with, "Well…" and then grin radiantly as she looked at our faces. Though soft-spoken, her words were powerful, and she exuded excitement about any new discovery from the lessons. Alice loved my over-zealous enthusiasm to learn about Jesus, and she encouraged me to continue seeking Him. She became like a grandmother to me, and I knew she was a gift from God.

As I continued studying Jonah, I could see how I had run from God. Like Jonah, God had found me and brought me back. Through the steady preaching and teaching that I received at Dillon Community Church, I joyfully received the good news and learned that the Word was alive and active, sharper than any double-edged sword (Hebrews 4:12). I now had purpose, meaning and someone to live for—Jesus Christ!

I began writing devotions and journals about all that I was discovering as I read the Bible. I also started to become more involved in the life of the church, helping out with the high school youth group and taking part in other Bible studies.

James, however, did not share my enthusiasm. Though he attended church when he could out of duty, we were not on the same page. My relentless questioning and invitations to come to church often landed us in battles and further frustrations, so I learned to back off.

We had longstanding arguments about the dishes. I should have known before marrying him that he would not wash them, because his apartment in Banner Elk was covered in dirty dishes. Sometimes I'd spot a mouse running through. Often he'd buy paper plates so he wouldn't have to clean them. Nevertheless, my anger burned when I'd come home after a long day of work to find dirty dishes piled high. Yet as I started pursuing Jesus and read passages such as 1 Peter 3:1 that says, "you wives, be submissive to your own husbands so that even if any of them are disobedient to the word, they may be won without a word by the behavior of their wives." I knew I had to put off the old self, those self-motivated patterns of thinking, and put on the new. I began doing the dishes, at first in a begrudging way, but it soon turned into a sweet time. I started using dishwashing time to pray or sing to Jesus. Rather than hate, love stirred my heart to serve my husband. This was a lesson that I continued learning again and again. I couldn't win my husband to Christ by pressuring him to come to church. I had to love him, just as Christ had wooed me.

He still threatened to leave on occasion, but I continued to stand my ground. Like Jonah arriving in Nineveh, I knew I was exactly where I was supposed to be because I had finally taken the first step of obedience. As much as I enjoyed all the adventures that James and I shared during our first years of marriage, I realized that I had neglected making space for those calm floats with my first love, Jesus Christ.

> *I had neglected making space for those calm floats with my first love, Jesus Christ.*

God continued to transform me as I spent time with Him. In my job with the Marriott Mountain Valley Lodge, I worked alongside several strong Christians who helped me pursue Christ and a life of holiness. Holiness was certainly a new word that never really stuck in my vocabulary, but I knew it was part of surrendering. Even James helped to point me toward purity by suggesting that I should stop watching shows like *Charmed,* which made witchcraft appear good. I began thoughtfully examining the media I was absorbing, which stuck to my brain like glue. It was hard, but like an old bandage, I was able to peel it off slowly.

I found out that Megan, a massage therapist at work, was a Christian, and she helped me turn away from the music that had become so rooted in my identity. Though I loathed letting it go, because it was a major part of my youth and friendships, the lyrics did not bring glory to God, and so I knew I had to get rid of it. I writhed when I first listened to Christian music on the radio as I drove to and from work. The beat, lyrics, and melodies seemed like watching a B-grade movie with amateur actors and poor quality production. But as I started to listen, I began to enjoy the music, and eventually, my old cassette tapes and CDs went into the trash.

Another Christian co-worker, Monica, was the housekeeping manager and though I had formerly called her a "Bible beater" under my breath because of the way she was always talking about God, I came to appreciate her bold faith. She used every opportunity to reach the nations, as most our housekeeping staff came from other countries, including Poland, Mexico, and many countries in Africa. I admired her spunk and fearlessness as she shared her faith.

Tia, who quietly and humbly worked at the front desk, had just graduated from high school. After I began talking to her about prayer, we began to pray together during our lunch breaks. During one of those prayer times, spiritual conversations came up with some of our non-Christian co-workers. One of the housekeepers was Muslim, and he explained how he was fasting during Ramadan. We asked what he thought of Jesus, and he said that he believed he was a prophet but not God. When this door opened in our conversation, we shared our beliefs about Jesus. When he left the room, we looked at each other with amazement about how the Lord had opened the door to plant a seed.

While my job at the Marriott began as the first step on a career ladder in hospitality, I realized that I had actually been given an assignment in God's kingdom. I began stirring up conversations about faith whenever I took people hiking or snowshoeing. When I called my mom to tell her about it, she told me to be careful, because she was nervous I might get fired. But that was the least of my worries, because Jesus was my first love, and when you are in love, you want to tell everyone you meet about Him. I had finally realized that my true "happily ever after" is in Jesus Christ, who laid down his life for us in love and invites us to do the same for Him.

Behold, you are beautiful, my love;
behold, you are beautiful;
your eyes are doves.
Behold, you are beautiful, my beloved, truly delightful.
Our couch is green; the beams of our house are cedar;
our rafters are pine.
—Song of Solomon 1:15–16
New American Standard Bible

~ 6 ~

HIS CHILDREN

W
HEN WATER LEVELS on the river change, the rapids transform completely. After settling in Colorado, the water levels began to rise, bringing surprising changes around the bends in the river ahead of us. We could neither anticipate nor prepare for these changes but had to paddle forward together. I now had a renewed understanding to trust God and that He would guide us and give us wisdom as we approached each new rapid.

2003–2005 (Summit County, Colorado)

With James often not around due to his crazy work schedule and his volunteer work at Summit County Search & Rescue, I longed for companionship and decided I wanted to get a puppy. James laughed when I shared my excitement with him. Despite his lack of enthusiasm about caring for a dog, I bought a puppy manual to learn how to raise one. Again, he chuckled and said, "No, we will not get a puppy." But I so wanted a friend, even if all he could do was bark back.

Around this same time, I decided to lose some weight and went on the new hit wonder, the Atkins diet, which recommended not using birth control pills in order to have maximum results. I hated taking those mood-swinging pills anyway. Sometimes I forgot to take one, or it would drop down the sink—*whoops*! So I stopped taking them, not really thinking about the consequences, since James had had cancer, and the doctors had always said he would never be able to have children because of all the heavy radiation. We never really talked about having kids. It just wasn't going to be a reality for us.

But after only a month or two, I felt funny, and sure enough, the little blue line appeared on the pregnancy test strip. Twenty-four years old, pregnant, and not even ready to raise a puppy, I cried, "Oh Lord, what am I going to do?" I had a failed track record as a babysitter—my first gig had ended up with a child in the ER after he scrambled across the porch ledge and fell. How in the world was I to handle my own?

I finally mustered up the courage to tell James. "Surprise! I'm pregnant!" I shared with a half-smile, wondering how he'd take the news. He responded with as much fret as I did. We both cried— tears of joy, but we were also freaking out!

The months ahead were filled with both excitement and pain. Every day, I'd get in the car to drive to work, start driving, and then I'd have to pull over to puke out the car door. Thankfully, by the time I arrived in Breckenridge, I was no longer sick. This went on daily for months.

As we began to prepare, the nine months never seemed like enough with all there was to do. We changed the "outdoor gear" room into a baby room with a baby blue color, as the evidence from the ultrasound clearly displayed I was carrying a boy. Our life was now focused on this new little life rather than ourselves. We said goodbye to hiking big peaks and being snob skiers (only skiing on powder days). We were going where we had never traveled before.

The day of the delivery, like most firsts, was long and grueling. I was in serious pain all night, and James kept telling me it was a false alarm and to go back to bed. I walked back and forth, gripping the couch, while my husband was sound asleep. After writhing in pain for several hours, he finally took me to the hospital, but it wasn't yet time. He was right, and so I had to continue waiting and waiting.

I was eventually put in a nice hospital room with a stereo system and a light wooden interior. Though it wasn't the Ritz Carlton, it was definitely better than a Motel 6. But as I felt the baby come, all the amenities meant nothing. All I could do was vomit—first onto the nurse, who looked at me in shock, and then straight onto the doctor's face. He had the nurse wipe his glasses so he could keep his hands ready for the catch. All I could say was, "I'm sorry." Having a child was just messy, but after the pain and the blood, Jake Austin Bennett—the most precious gift—emerged on April 27, 2003.

As soon as he came into the world, the doctor took him and then the nurse cleaned him up since he had pooped in the placenta. When his tiny body was clean, he reached up and grabbed his daddy's finger tightly. James was overjoyed to share the special bond of father and son with Jake. That story of Jake grabbing his father's finger would be told and retold many times. James was so proud to be a father.

That story of Jake grabbing his father's finger would be told and retold many times.

I stayed in the hospital, and the staff taught me many things about how to care for a baby. When Jake arrived, I honestly wondered, *What am I supposed to do?* I was completely oblivious except for the training I received pre-birth, and so the nurses taught me how to wrap him in a blanket, breastfeed, and burp him. When we finally left the hospital, James and I panicked as we strapped little Jake into the car seat. We were both terrified that he wouldn't make it home, because we were so nervous to be new parents taking care of this new life. He was so vulnerable and fragile, and we didn't want to mess up.

We were living over 9,000 feet above sea level, and so I had to leave the hospital with an oxygen tank, because Jake didn't adapt well to the altitude. Wherever I went, I had to tote around the heavy tank along with all the baby gear, and so we stayed inside most of the time. The slippery parking lot and roads from heavy snow that spring made leaving even more challenging.

Motherhood didn't come naturally to me, and no matter how many books I read or how much advice I received, I was challenged daily. Depression sunk in, and while I sunk, James invested more and more time in rescue missions and hanging out at bars with other volunteers on the squad. He started attending more trainings, sometimes all day on Saturdays, to learn about technical rescues.

I was completely surprised when I found out he drank his first beer after all those years of being sober. He had vowed he would never drink again, and yet when I saw him sitting in the recliner with a beer in his hand, he shrugged it off. But I knew better. I'm sure I gave him a look and said a few words. He shot arrows right back at me. *This will not have a good ending*, I thought.

One beer a night became two beers and then three. He had always been so strong, drinking soda rather than alcohol, but wanting to fit in and for reasons I'll never know, he lost sight of his priorities.

One night, he asked me if he could go to a bachelor's party, and I said, "Yes." I still believed my husband was tough enough to keep his moral convictions and do what was right for our family. He went, leaving Jake and me at home. We slept through the night, but James had an all-night drinking fest with his buddies that included some hard liquor.

The morning after the party, he arrived home a nervous wreck. He appeared as if he had been in a car accident, as he shook while explaining what had happened. Panicked and jittery, I tried to calm him down to figure out what was the matter. Later, I would come to understand that he had been experiencing an anxiety attack. He explained how the party had had strippers, excessive drinking, and his worst nightmare kept spinning over and over in his head. He was having an obsessive, compulsive fear that some of the other people there had done something to harm him. But I knew it wasn't true. I was deeply convinced nothing happened, but he was just as convinced that something horrible happened to him.

For months, I listened to the same story repeated like an old country song, with the same lyrics played over and over. I reassured him that what he thought had happened didn't happen, because he was completely wasted that night. He talked to me about the incident daily and then invested a lot of money into audiotapes to help relieve the stress and relax his mind. The tapes instructed him about how to breathe and calm down. I could've taught him that from Lamaze class, but he was desperate and jumped on whatever he could find.

After that experience, he never drank another alcoholic beverage again. I started to feel like we were drawing closer. Though he continued to invest in Search & Rescue, he avoided all the social life at the bars. Slowly, James was learning to embrace his new role as a dad and slowly coming back to me.

With that episode behind us, we decided to move out of our condo and try to make income from our sweat equity. We got a realtor, put it on the market, and waited. Days, weeks, months, and then an entire year rolled by. There was not even one bid. We found a new realtor, Dan, who volunteered on the Search & Rescue team and went to our church (he wasn't one of his former drinking buddies). After asking him to sell the place, it sold within months, but the $1,000 we made was far less than we expected, as the cost of our extreme makeover was more than that. As it turns out, a tire blew out going to the closing, and we had to replace all the tires on our all-wheel drive Subaru, which cost exactly $1,000. Though we didn't make any money on our condo, I was grateful for the way God provided for our needs.

We moved to Dillon, Colorado only a few miles from our condo in Wilderness and lived in the basement of a home close to the church. Even though we were in the basement, it was such a bright place, since Lake Dillon was right outside our door, and we had windows in every room where the sun shone through.

At the same time, I continued to grow in faith. I finished reading the Bible for the first time and approached Pastor Mark and asked excitedly, "What do I do now?" He replied, "Keep reading" and gave me an Inductive Bible study by Precept Ministries. I was overjoyed to have this study Bible to keep growing in God's Word and promised Mark that I would keep reading and studying. For nearly eight years, I went through that particular study day after day. Years later, I learned the founder of Precept Ministries, Kay Arthur, went to First Presbyterian Church in Tennessee, which was my church while growing up. Kay had also been my mom's best friend's Sunday school teacher.

While I was growing in my understanding of Jesus, James and I got another surprise—another blue strip! As this new baby girl grew inside me, I felt a growing desire to be baptized. From reading the Word, I understood that wouldn't save me, but would declare publicly what was happening inside of me—new life. As a child of the King, I wanted to obey.

Weeks before my baptism, I invited my co-workers at the Marriott to share this celebration. Some of them may have thought I was obnoxious, but I was so full of joy in the Lord that I couldn't contain it. Months into my second pregnancy, I took the plunge to demonstrate my death to sin and my resurrection in new life in Jesus Christ. As I stood dripping wet with a big belly and full of life, I wanted to tell everyone about how Jesus had made me into a new creation.

I wanted to name my daughter Elizabeth as a reflection of the joy I was experiencing. I felt like Elizabeth when she was pregnant with John the Baptist, and he leaped in her womb with joy when Mary greeted her. Today, when I say my daughter's name (whom we now call Lizzy), I still remember the incredible experience we shared together, even though she was not yet born, and I recall the story of Elizabeth meeting Mary and being filled with joy and the Holy Spirit.

Elizabeth Jayne Bennett arrived on January 24, 2005 as a special blessing. The ladies from the church poured into our lives, bringing meals for weeks and lavishing us with a baby shower and gifts. They took us in like family, since our own families were far away, and truly practiced what they preached.

Observing the love of these women, James reflected, "It's interesting how you invested your time into the church, and look at what we've received. I invested my time in Search & Rescue, and not one person has come to visit." This triggered James to start thinking about how we could do more for God, which came as a shock because he always hemmed and hawed about going to church. I loved the way he was growing in love with Jesus. He even thought up the name for a future ministry organization: Search & Rescue for Souls. He wondered how our love for the outdoors could become a launching pad to tell others about Jesus.

While we dreamed, we were also facing reality. We couldn't afford to live in Colorado, paying for two children in childcare at nearly $1,400 per child per month. Childcare was more expensive than our rental expense, and there was no way to survive on one income so I could stay at home to care for them. To solve this problem, we decided to move back to Tennessee to be close to my family. We'd live with my parents for a few months, land decent jobs, and then find an affordable home in Chattanooga. Maybe along the way, we could make our ministry dream a reality.

So soon after Lizzy was born and weaned, I submitted my resignation to the Marriott Mountain Valley Lodge, and James resigned from his job. After five years in Colorado, we packed a U-Haul and headed back east, full of excitement for the next adventure, but also grieving the loss of our incredible church family at Dillon Community Church and the adventurous lifestyle we'd had at our fingertips in Summit County. But we knew it was time to shed our selfish desires and focus on raising Jake and Lizzy.

Of course, plans often change, as I had already learned on the unforgiving river of my life thus far: Brandon's death, my expectations of a "happily ever after" marriage, and now two little miracles in our midst. But Jake and Lizzy would change the course of our lives—not only through our physical relocation, but also our spiritual formation. Their humility and childlike faith has taught me more about Jesus than anyone else. As their parent, I learned about the Father heart of God and God's radical, unconditional love. I also came to understand how discipline is an expression of that love and how I needed to become like a child as I returned to God. My children have been gifts from the Lord, drawing me closer to Him through their powerful bedtime prayers and simple but incredible belief in a big God who is the giver of life.

Behold, children are a gift from the Lord;
The fruit of the womb is a reward.
—Psalm 127:3
New American Standard 1977

~ 7 ~

HIS TENTS

RIVERS ARE IN a state of constant change because of the elements and the environment that surrounds them. When storms pass through, they leave debris and can change the water's path. The rocks become smooth from the force of the powerful waters rushing over them. As our stakes moved from place to place in our early marriage, we learned how to adapt and, more importantly, I learned to depend on God as we ventured beyond the thrill of riding rapids into new territories and seasons.

2005–2006 (Tennessee to Idaho)

Our time in Tennessee turned out to be a wilderness experience, as we were not able to find work, and we struggled to find a church home. Though we had planned to live with my parents for three months, we ended up living with them for a year and a half. With a baby and a toddler, our time together became a trial for all of us. James was desperate to find work and finally took a night job delivering newspapers. In distress, I applied to the insurance company call center where my dad had worked. Having searched for so long for employment, we were discouraged about not finding jobs to support Jake and Lizzy, and we were also missing Colorado. Like the children of Israel, we became complainers and asked God why He had allowed us to return home only to find nothing. In reflecting on this season of our life together much later, I realized that we were being pruned and tested.

Though the job at the insurance company was totally out of my gifting, I met some incredible people, and one co-worker was a strong Christian. When there were no calls, we talked and spurred each other on in the faith. We were trained to spend only a few minutes per phone call and were rated on this in our performance review, but when I received a call from a woman who had lost her health, job, friends, and family, I could not hang up. She was completely hopeless and had no one else to talk to, and I had only been trained to answer questions about claims and connect the caller to the right person. The woman almost sounded suicidal, and so I just sat there and listened for an hour. The call reminded me that it's not a career or the money we make that's most important, but somehow James and I both lost sight of that along the way.

After six months working there, I found another job at a local university, working in continuing education. Though different from my tourism background, it certainly didn't have the rigidity of a call center and would allow me to get a master's degree at no cost. I found another "light" in the university office in Cheryl, who always greeted me in the mornings with a glowing smile. Though I struggled to fit into the team there, Cheryl had been there for more than fifteen years and encouraged me.

Within my first ninety days at the university, Lizzy became frequently ill. I had to drive an hour from my parents' house in South Pittsburg to her childcare, but whenever she had a high fever, they would refuse to keep her, and so I would leave work to come pick her up. Though I missed many days of work because of her sickness, my manager always encouraged me that being a mom was more important. I tried to maximize my benefits by starting a master's degree in business and took an economics class and an accounting class.

A few days a week, I woke up at 4 a.m. to go for an hour run, and I'd always imagine that the long country road to my parent's house was the final leg of my race in life. I imagined the ribbon I needed to run through to win and pressed forward. I cherished those runs as I prayed and thought and worked through my disappointment about having to live with my parents and not being where I had envisioned we would be in life. Living in Tennessee felt like we had taken steps backward, but I wanted to keep moving forward.

After arriving back home after those runs, I'd do homework for school before waking up the children to take the long drive to childcare and work. Though I enjoyed my classes, business wasn't my favorite subject. Reading the *Wall Street Journal* for accounting and learning about micro and macroeconomics wasn't exactly my cup of tea, but I imagined it would lead towards a better ending.

With all the demands of work and schooling on top of raising a family, I felt like I hit a wall when my manager and her director pulled me into the office one day, sat me down, and then shared that they were letting me go. Shocked, I burst into tears, and then my manager started to cry, too. I'd had too many absences in that first ninety-day window. Though I'd managed to get my work done, they had decided I just did not fit the team.

I left the campus mortified, as I had never been fired from a job since I had started working at the age of fourteen. I had always been a model employee, and in school I had always been a hard worker and fought for A's. I wondered why we had ever left Colorado. Though I was living in my hometown of Chattanooga, I felt like a foreigner, completely rejected, as if the city was trying to spit us out.

I became angry as I contemplated what our family would do. I spent day after day filling out applications, pulling out my hair to find the perfect career and do my best with the education my parents had sacrificed to give me. But finding a job had consumed my life, and it was an idol that needed to be cut down. Pruning was not something I enjoyed, but I needed some major trimming.

Standing on the porch to the apartment above my parents' garage, the pressure brewing inside me exploded, and I stomped outside and screamed at God in bitterness. I was like my toddler, pounding my fists and pointing my finger to tell Him exactly how I felt. After my outbreak, I realized my need to repent. I had stepped out of line too many times, and I was only craving what I wanted rather than seeking to know what God wanted. Like the Israelites complaining about the manna from heaven, I was complaining even though I had everything I needed—food to eat, a home to stay in, and a family who loved me.

As I began to cool off, my hope tank started to fill back up. One day, as I was filling out yet another application, I asked James, "Where do you think we should go?" With certainty, he replied, "I think Idaho," and then he encouraged me to apply anywhere in the U.S.A., not just in Chattanooga or the Southeast.

After submitting twenty, then thirty, applications, I decided to take some time to enjoy scrapbooking with my mom. At first I didn't want to leave my computer, but in my spirit, I knew it was where God wanted me to be. So I went to the main house, and it turned out to be the most wonderful day. I finally felt relief as if the heavy burdens had been lifted off my shoulders. My mom and I cut paper, talked, and pasted while the kids played. In the middle of our activities, the University of Idaho phoned and asked to interview me for a position in their recreation department. They even offered to fly me there.

With excitement, I boarded the plane and headed to the Northwest, a place I had always dreamed of going. I rented a car and was amazed by the countryside as I drove to Moscow, passing lush green hills without any trees in sight. Then I saw a vast and deep canyon out in the middle of nowhere, glowing as the sun set. I couldn't believe that God had brought me to such a place, as for so long, I had been sitting in the little apartment above my parents' garage, hopeless and stuck.

I went to the recreation department and was shocked by the size of the facility. I sat with an older man, who told me tales of sailing in the Pacific Ocean, and his wild adventures reminded me of my old river guiding buddies on the Ocoee. Then I headed to a restaurant to meet two men to interview for the job. The interview went okay, but I wasn't sure if this was the right place for our family. If we were going to move across the country again, I was hoping we'd be in the mountains.

Then I took a long excursion from Moscow to Sandpoint, Idaho to interview at the Chamber of Commerce. While I had been looking for jobs, I had talked to a woman at this office, who had been so welcoming as she answered my questions. She invited me to share my background and describe the work I was seeking and then encouraged me to apply for a position with the Chamber, but they had been hesitant to hire me without an interview. When I found out I'd be flown to Moscow, I took the opportunity to drive to Sandpoint and interview with the Chamber. When I crossed the Long Bridge over the waters of Lake Pend Oreille, I could see the endless chain of mountains, and it felt like home. As I drove around the quaint downtown with local stores, I noticed little espresso stands on every corner. This was the Northwest that I had imagined.

The interview took place at the Chamber office in an old building next to Sand Creek, where I had a magnificent view of kayakers out the window. I interviewed well, then headed back to the airport to fly to Tennessee. I wasn't offered the job at the university, but the Chamber hired me on a part-time basis at minimum wage.

Though the pay was low, James and I decided to take the risk, and so we packed another U-Haul, feeling confident that we were in the center of God's will, and headed off on a four-day drive to Sandpoint with our two little bundles of joy. We drove through the Midwest, the wild Dakotas and the entire state of Montana, staying at cheap KOAs along the way and taking frequent bathroom breaks for the little ones. It was a very long journey, but we finally arrived in Sandpoint in the northern tip of Idaho's panhandle.

With no place to stay, we found a campground at Round Lake State Park, and our tent became a temporary home for the next two weeks as we looked for a more permanent residence. Again, I was reminded of the trek of the Israelites who lived in tents in the wilderness and were reminded of God's care for them whenever they celebrated the Feast of Booths. "'You shall live in booths for seven days. . . so that your generations may know that I had the sons of Israel live in booths when I brought them out from the land of Egypt. I am the LORD your God'" (Leviticus 23:42–43 NASB). Though we lived through some rough times, He was taking care of us.

Every morning I chuckled as I dressed professionally for work, first cleaning off my toes, which were caked in dirt from stepping in the mud after my shower. After a few days of going to work, I felt terrible leaving James behind, as he had to suffer with Jake and Lizzy in the intense heat, changing diapers, cooking over the camp fire, and calming them through their constant toddler moments.

Although James loved tents and camping, it was becoming excruciating for him with Jake and Lizzy, and eventually we found a condo to rent on Schweitzer Mountain for a week. Though the price was high, it was worth it for James and the kids. Once again, God provided for us, and I saw a glimmer of the bigger picture. Though I had lost my job in Tennessee, God was stretching my understanding so that I could see a panoramic view. Finally, I could see the mountaintops beyond the valley.

Moving to Sandpoint was not what I planned or expected, but it was a gift. God rescued me from that treacherous season in Tennessee, but He used it to tear down some idols that I was holding tightly. By grace, He pruned me and continued the good work He had started. As God led me along rocky roads and through wild terrain, I got a lot of scraped knees, but He taught me about His sovereignty and provision. Through it all, I was drawing closer to the great I AM, who led the children of Israel to the promise land. Just as He worked in them, He was transforming my heart to reflect His nature. I was learning that "home" is not a physical place with brick and mortar, or even a tarp with poles, but my true home is under the shelter of the Most High.

He who dwells in the shelter of the Most High
will abide in the shadow of the Almighty.
—Psalm 91:1
New American Standard Bible

~ 8 ~

HIS FELLOWSHIP

O N THE RIVER, there is a special camaraderie among river guides (or river dwellers, as we used to call ourselves), as we share a common interest in the wild, adventure, and risk. However, this camaraderie cannot compare to the community of Jesus Christ and his followers. As our family followed the winding turns of our life together, God led us around a bend that brought us unexpectedly to the Northwest. On this journey, He placed me in fellowship with many saints in Sandpoint, who challenged and strengthened my faith in unique ways. They built me up and trained me to depend on Jesus before being led to the next frontier.

2006-2010 (Sandpoint, Idaho)

With snow-covered peaks surrounding the massive Lake Pend Oreille, Sandpoint is an incredibly beautiful paradise. The lake is forty-five miles long, and heavy winds churn up waves as choppy as those in the sea. Whenever I traveled the long bridge across the lake, I took in the panoramic view, taking pictures with my eyes over and over. We felt like we were making our new home in this amazing place, which seemed to fit our whole family. During the summer, we put Jake and Lizzy in backpacks and hiked up the trails; in winter, we helped them find their ski legs at Schweitzer Mountain Ski Resort.

But I had learned that no place could become a true home until we nestled in the community by finding a church. That first year was difficult as we scrambled from place to place, looking for both a church home and a place to live. We finally found an affordable apartment complex near the library, and it just so happened to be in the backyard of First Christian Church. The convenient location suited us all.

Though running continued to be therapeutic for me, I ran less and less because of the brutal Sandpoint winters. It was extremely difficult to get out of bed when all I wanted to do was wrap my hands around a hot cup of coffee. Throughout that first winter, I somehow managed to keep running about once each week through snow, ice, and bone-chilling winds. But as the sun came up, it warmed my frostbitten fingers and soggy feet, which got wet when I accidentally ran over thin ice and then crunched into freezing water. The picturesque sunrises reflecting orange over Lake Pend Oreille or peeking through the dark valleys filled me with awe and wonder and swept away my discomfort from the bitter cold. I continued to run through Sandpoint with gratitude and joy as often as I could.

Though working for pay was essential for our family's economic survival, work life always divided us. James and I never had the same schedules because we couldn't afford full-time childcare, and so we were always pulled in various directions. After settling in Sandpoint, James got a job at Schweitzer Mountain, working night shifts in security, and so he was always absent or asleep when we were together.

We found childcare for Lizzy and Jake with a woman who cared for children in her home, but we were the only family with two parents since the rest of the children came from single-parent homes. I was always astounded to hear the stories from the other moms who were working two or three jobs at fast-food restaurants, bagging groceries, or other odd jobs just to get by. While James and I had our struggles, we had one another to lean upon, and yet sometimes I felt a bit like those single moms.

In my job at the Chamber, I was constantly learning about Sandpoint and shaking hands with influential people, from Congressmen and mayors to CEOs and small business owners. As a transplant, I had to figure out who was who and all the changes in community development. Our office had a visitor center, and so I also had to learn about tourism in the area. While tending administrative work in the back office, I constantly had to pop out to answers tourists' questions about where they should go and what they should do. I loved the change and variety, and for the first time, I had a job that combined my love for tourism with community development. In creating this new position, my boss, Judy, included communications in my role. I started writing press releases to promote businesses and building relationships with the editor of the local paper. I also learned about graphic design as I created various promotional pieces for Chamber events and workshops. I felt that God had blessed me with this tailor-made job.

Judy, the executive director, was an incredibly hard worker and was constantly pulled in many directions, but she taught me how to navigate the small world of Sandpoint and helped me grow as a professional. Our little all-female team became like a family, and we internally called ourselves the "Chamber Chicks."

When Judy resigned, I really didn't want her to go, but the Chamber hired someone from the corporate office of Coldwater Creek not far from our office, who had a love for the nonprofit world and needed a change. In the end, I loved working for the new executive director, Amy, as much as I had loved working for Judy. Amy liked change, and she wasn't held back by bureaucracy or old thinking. She shifted and moved the organization and also shook things up for me by allowing me to start the first youth leadership program. At the same time, Amy emphasized work and life balance. When Amy saw me working after hours to prepare for the next meeting, write a newsletter, or build a new program, she would say, "Heather, you need to go home." A working mother herself, she was always mindful of my hours. If we had an event that required a ten-hour day, she would make sure we took time off the next day or later in the week. Her motto was, "Heather, we're not saving lives." These words stuck like a Post-it note on my mind, and I continued to remember them in the years ahead. Though I thought I had learned the lesson about making an idol of work in Tennessee, I clearly hadn't—but Amy helped me remember my priorities.

Outside of my fast-paced working life, Jake, Lizzy, and I attended a local church, but we always sat with a vacancy because James was so often fast asleep on Sunday mornings. I desperately wanted him with us and prayed that one day our family would be able to attend church together. In the meantime, God was leading me to people who helped me to grow in the depths of God's Word and in wisdom on how to live out my faith boldly.

God was leading me to people who helped me grow in the depths of God's Word and in wisdom on how to live out my faith boldly.

I quickly began looking for a small group within our church and plugged into one that had a mix of couples and singles. I always appreciated having singles, since I knew James would not be coming. Our group met in a beautiful home each week and went through a Bible study or Bible curriculum. One of my favorites was the *Truth Project,* which was designed to give us a better biblical worldview.

I immediately connected with Teri, another Sandpoint newbie who had recently moved with her husband from California. She and her husband, Rick, had been active members at Saddleback Church, and their servant hearts were evident. Her zeal for the Lord Jesus was contagious. Excited and passionate, I wanted to hang out more with her, which, in looking back, revealed my desire for discipleship. With a clear gift of leadership and encouragement, she became an incredible witness and fanned the flame in my own journey to know Jesus.

We began meeting at her home or the local coffee shop when she had time in between her hectic job in corporate retail. I marveled at the way she shared Jesus through her position, showing her employees and co-workers love through the candy jar on her desk and many other ways. Rather than holding fast to her own position and authority, she gave it away. Eventually, she made her department so efficient that she ended up working herself out of a job, reflecting Jesus' leadership style of equipping and empowering his disciples. Her faith shined like gold to all around her.

She fanned the flame in me, too, and I began sharing with her about my passion to reach people who had never heard the gospel, to start a women's Bible study at our church, and to bring local Christian musicians into the coffee shop. Rather than blowing off my dreams and ideas, she kept blowing on the spark and encouraging me until it caught.

Teri stood by my side as I began taking steps of faith. The first step I took was to organize a Bible study on the book of Daniel. Twenty women attended, and Teri was there with me from start to finish. I then took another step and asked the manager of the local Starbucks if we could invite Christian artists to play. To my surprise, he agreed, and so I invited several Christian artists to play. While the numbers were few, Rick and Teri were there to support me, saying, "We're here for you, Heather. Keep going, girl!" They always gave me big grins, bear hugs, and expressed their enthusiasm for my faith journey. I later heard about the term "spiritual parents" and realized that Teri and Rick had become those for me.

I continued to grow in faith and to be encouraged by others. I met some women (and occasionally a brave man or two) at a small Christian writer's group, which was comprised of people who had many more years of experience than me, some published and others on the way. We sent our one-hundred-word count essays to the group, and then we'd gather at Anita's house to share our critiques on each other's pieces.

Anita had a spunky, cheerful personality, and she always greeted us at the door with warmth and hospitality. Her short red hair fit her personality. We'd enter to the aroma of hot tea or coffee and hear the cats purring around the corner. We'd sit around the wooden dining room table, chit chat about the latest in Sandpoint, sip on our hot drinks, pray and then discuss our writing. I always felt like a novice, but I cherished these times together.

Terese, another member of the writer's group, had long gray hair and a tan face from her life outdoors—riding her bike, trail running, swimming, blueberry picking, and a little bit of everything in between. After raising her three sons, homeschooling and then teaching in a local private school, she went to school for her teaching certification. She was always laughing and living fully, but as a woman of the Word, she was also deep and wise.

One day, she surprised me by asking, "Heather, what would you think if I were to do an internship with you?" My head spun. *How could she do an internship with me? I should do an internship with her on how to be a godly woman, wife, and mother!* Even though I resisted because of my age, she persisted, and our friendship took root.

Even though I was her internship supervisor at the Chamber, she taught me so much about life, faith, athletics, motherhood, and grace. Her motherly love was a testimony in our office. Sometimes she'd bring a brown bag full of fresh cherries from her cherry tree, which was my first experience eating raw cherries, as I had grown up thinking that cherries were bright red and came in a jar full of syrup—*yuk*! They always disgusted me until I tried the real fresh fruit. Terese also brought us homemade chocolate chip cookies, which she made from scratch. Every once and a while, she'd share a secret about how to keep the cookies soft and the importance of using real butter instead of margarine.

We shared life together both in and outside the office. Sometimes we'd run by the lake on the trails, and though I knew she could go faster, she would graciously run at a slower pace for me. We'd walk around the park with my kids, discussing life and faith while my kids played on the slides. She became another "spiritual mom," teaching me about how to be a godly wife and mother as she was navigating her new role as a mother-in-law.

I also met Tracy the summer that I facilitated the Bible study on Daniel at our church. My mom had come out to visit, and I had to work at the Taste of Sandpoint, one of our biggest fundraisers, so I recruited my mom to fill in for me at the study. After meeting Tracy, my mom insisted that I call her, because she knew we would be great friends.

Tracy and I were both in the same stages of life. She was married and had a son named Aiden who was about the same age as my daughter, and so we immediately connected. We started meeting at her house so our kids could get to know each other and play. During the summer months, they played in the backyard, swung on the tire swing hanging from a tree, picked berries out of her garden, played with their chickens, or played with cool science toys in Aiden's room. While the kids played, we sat at her dining room table, sipping on freshly brewed coffee from big mugs, talking for hours about books, world events, local news, motherhood, and discussing all these things through the lens of Scripture. By the time our conversation had to end, my mug would have just a little bit of cold coffee remaining. It felt like the time was never long enough.

As all these friendships grew, I was growing, too, but James had only a few relationships, although one godly man spoke into his life during the wee hours of work. The old habits I had seen when he was volunteering with the search and rescue team in Dillon were taking root. James began isolating himself, and I knew from our conversations that social situations were incredibly difficult for him. Because he didn't have a college education and had to work in low-wage, low-level jobs, he stayed away from intimate relationships beyond our family. He felt we were his community, and that was good enough for him. He dreaded questions about what he did for a living because they reminded him that he was a failure by his own standards. Though the kids and I never saw him that way, it was hard to convince James to see himself differently. It was easier for James to be a loner and retreat from society, but I had chosen another path. I longed for a rich community where I was surrounded by others, accepted and dependent upon God and His family.

At church, I wanted to get more involved, and so I approached Pastor Kyle and told him that I could serve anywhere. With a friendly smile, he told me that they could use help in the children's ministry, which was definitely not what I had in mind. I immediately agreed, but I went away a bit disappointed.

When I approached the children's ministry team the first day, they were busy tending all the three to five year-olds as they arrived in the class. At the time, Jake and Lizzy fell in this age bracket, and so it was a perfect fit for me to be with them. I escorted Jake and Lizzy through the entrance and down the hallway to one of the classrooms, and then I met each volunteer. As I met each person, I realized I was meeting Kyle's family. I met Katie, his wife, then Ethel Ann, his grandmother, and then Bill, his dad, and then Roberta, his mom. Roberta had short, bright red hair, which perfectly fit her petite frame. Anna and Dawn were the only volunteers who weren't related to Pastor Kyle.

Despite my negative attitude, I started enjoying my time with the children week after week. Cutting paper to make sheep, pouring gold fish for snacks in little colored cups, and singing with their off-tune, cracked voices became a delight. Beside me, Jake and Lizzy were learning and growing in the Lord.

Roberta, the leader, did not show her age, as she had remained active and lived a healthy lifestyle like most Northwest women. Her tiny figure reflected strength rather than weakness. She was firm but gentle, watching after the children as if they were her very own. She always made sure the bottom half of the split-door was closed to the hallway so that children would not wander off. If anyone had to go to the bathroom, she made sure they had an escort to the door. When the parents came, she guided each child by the hand. When Roberta was around, everything was orderly— even if the small room was packed with thirty children.

One day while there was a moment of quiet, I asked, "What's your secret? How did you raise a son like Kyle?" I wanted to know every little tidbit she could give me, not only as a mother, but a wife, too. During our short conversations when I could ask these questions, I learned about her influence in her own husband's life. Her husband wasn't always serving alongside her, which was a glimmer of hope for me, since I couldn't fathom James stepping foot into the children's ministry, much less serving in the church.

She told me that she had made her home the place for all the kids to come. She chuckled as she reminded me to have lots of food, especially for the boys, when they become teenagers. She also shared how she acted as a friend to her children's friends, inviting them to talk to her about anything.

We continued to serve alongside each other for another year. I didn't know Roberta very well, as we were always busy with kids, but I observed her strong example in how she loved those kids. There was always someone who needed to go to the potty, cups of water to fill, crafts that needed to be prepared, puppet shows to run, songs to sing, and little hearts that needed shepherding. She was like a mom to all of us.

One day, after the children were gone, Roberta lifted her shirt a little to show me her stomach and explained that something was going wrong. I placed my hand on her shoulder and said confidently, "You'll be okay." With my still immature faith, I just thought whatever was wrong would go away. I didn't even pray for her in that moment.

I didn't see Roberta the next week or the week after. As time went by, her family started to disappear from the children's ministry, because Roberta was fighting colon cancer. I continued to think that this would soon be over and her family would return, but they didn't. Weeks turned to months. Then on a Sunday in February 2008, I heard the news that Roberta had died. I had never gone to see her at the hospital. I was overwhelmed with regret and deep sadness. After the service, I wondered how I'd face the children during the children's ministry time. They often asked about Roberta, and it broke my heart to think that they would not see her again. It crushed me to think that her family would never see her on this side of eternity. I thought, *of all people, why Roberta?*

When I went home and spoke to James about Roberta, he consoled me, but he didn't understand the depth of the loss I felt. I was regretting the things I had never said, the prayers I had never prayed, the questions I hadn't asked, and the visit I had never made to say goodbye.

As I thought about Roberta, I often thought about the shepherd who carried "the rod" in Psalm 23. I had often struggled over that verse, because I thought of the rod as a whip or tool of punishment, but later I came to realize the rod was used to protect the sheep from wolves. Though the rod might hurt the sheep a bit, its purpose was to protect the sheep, like the parent who pulls a child away from a busy street. We can so wander away from Jesus, our guide, just like the child who loses his mom in the endless rows at WalMart, but the Good Shepherd wants to lead each of us back to a place of comfort and oversight by our heavenly Father's side. Roberta mirrored Jesus, our Good Shepherd, by guiding and protecting those little ones, her family, and her community.

More than eight hundred people came to the celebration of Roberta's life. Roberta had lived a life for Jesus and exemplified Him in the way she raised her children, loved her husband, served her family in Christ, and lived her faith in her work in the local high school. I lined up to say my condolences, and as I hugged Pastor Kyle, my heart sank for his entire family.

From that moment, God began to fan the flame in me to go out of my comfort zone and live. I kept meeting with Teri, who spurred me on, and when I wasn't sure of my calling, she emboldened me to give it a try.

One day a man who served in our church's worship team named Kevin phoned me. He had heard about the musicians at Starbucks and asked if I might be willing to work with their Christian band. When I learned about the band and their desire to make an album and play around town, I began taking a day off work so that I could help them find venues. As a novice, I started receiving small business coaching from the Idaho Small Business Development Center in Post Falls to glean wisdom about how to support this small enterprise. The director, Bill, was a former pastor, and one of his volunteer coaches was also a former pastor, and so I was shepherded by a man of God who understood biblical wisdom and leadership principals. When I began meeting with the band, I asked about their prayer life as a team, and when they said it wasn't strong, I encouraged them in that.

But I was struggling to find venues where they could play, and so Kevin suggested we have a concert at our church. We found two other artists and worked on promoting the concert to the community. We called it the "Unity Concert," as the hope was for many different denominations within the city to come together to praise and worship Jesus Christ. Around four hundred people attended, and in addition to the music, there were testimonies shared.

After the concert, Kevin arranged to record an album. We went to a nearby studio where popular artists had recorded. But the band was comprised of members from various life stages—one with a baby, another single, another retired, others with young kids and older kids—and they weren't ready to go on tour. One member ended up dropping out, and eventually the band dissipated.

While it didn't work out, one thing that struck me was the importance of prayer. I began to pray for our city like I never had before. I'd pace back and forth on the top floor of our office at the Chamber during lunch breaks or go to the park across the street and write my prayers. I later would see many churches gathering at that same park to pray for the city. It was really overwhelming to see God move in this little town that was often described as having much spiritual darkness.

Then I met a teenager named Holly who was also passionate about prayer. We started joining each other every Sunday during the church service to pray. Eventually, other prayer warriors joined in, and we became a small but mighty group, meeting in a small room upstairs above the children's ministry. It felt like a small glimpse of the disciples meeting in the upper room. During our prayer times, I felt like we were living into Paul's exhortation to the Hebrews: "Let us hold fast the confession of our hope without wavering, for He who promised is faithful; and let us consider how to stimulate one another to love and good deeds, not forsaking our own assembling together, as is the habit of some, but encouraging one another; and all the more, as you see the day drawing near" (Hebrews 10:23–25 NASB). After weeks of prayer, we began a Bible study about the power of the Holy Spirit. As part of the study, we watched videos with people from around the world. One video showed myriad Africans praising the name of Jesus, and I wept, deeply touched by the movement of God stirring on that continent, around the world, and in our small group in Sandpoint. While I prayed for big things, my deepest yearning was for James to love and passionately pursue Jesus.

One day as I fell prostrate on our living room floor in prayer, and I saw this picture of my kids walking with my friend Terese up a dark stairway, what appeared to be inside an old garage. I wanted to open my eyes, as it didn't seem pleasant; but then suddenly through their eyes, I opened the door as they yelled, "Surprise!" It was my birthday. Then in the back corner I saw James who appeared old, unengaged, and sat in the corner. After that, I realized that even though James wasn't involved with the celebratory occasion, I needed to keep living. More birthdays would come. In some ways it was giving me a glimpse of what was ahead, as James would not always be there with us and my friend Terese would be present for my kids and I in profound ways to help us put more birthday candles on the cake.

In Sandpoint, God used so many people to stimulate me towards love and good deeds. I continued to learn to let go of the idol of work, to serve where God sent me rather than where I wanted to serve and to pray fervently. Through my fellowship with the body of Christ, I was encouraged in love to mature in my faith over coffee, through lessons from the workplace, and many Post-it notes from a heavenly vantage point.

But after four years in Sandpoint, my spirit began to stir to move again. James felt it, too. Once again, I asked James where he thought we should go. I was thinking Seattle or Portland, but he was thinking Spokane. Though it was not my first pick, I knew it would be our next direction.

Rather, speaking the truth in love, we are to grow up in every way into him who is the head, into Christ, from whom the whole body, joined and held together by every joint with which it is equipped, when each part is working properly, makes the body grow so that it builds itself up in love.
—Ephesians 4:15–16
New American Standard Bible

~ 9 ~

HIS LEAD

W HEN NAVIGATING A river, if you let the powerful currents control your boat, you will be led to destruction. But if you use your paddle to fight against the powerful surge of water and follow the commands of an experienced guide, you will be set upon the right course. You just need to remain alert and ready, trusting that your guide knows what's best for you and everyone in the boat. As I embarked on my journey with James, I slowly learned to trust the voice of Jesus as my guide.

2010–2011 (Spokane, Washington)

When James and I got the itch to move again, I began looking for jobs in Spokane online and found a position as a small business program manager with Greater Spokane Incorporated. Thinking it might be a good fit, I submitted my cover letter and resume with James' approval, got an initial interview, and then I was called in for a second interview with the CEO.

The day of the second interview, James and I drove together from Idaho to Washington, about an hour and a half commute. When he dropped me off on busy Riverside Avenue, he leaned over and said, "I think this is it. I have a good feeling about this." I felt it, too.

I went to the reception and met a personable receptionist who had a distinct New York accent. She made me feel right at home in the sleek office with high walls painted in brilliant maroons and blue-grays, adorned with modern silver LD light fixtures. Our Chamber office in Idaho was in an old, rustic wooden building that had flooded and caused us to relocate our office. *Can I fit here?* I wondered. *Can I hang out with the elite of this city? I'm just a plain Jane from Tennessee.* Brushing those thoughts off my shoulders, I propelled myself forward in the confidence of James's words.

Sitting at a sleek desk with a corner office on the second floor overlooking the downtown streets of Spokane, I had a very brief interview, but left with the same feeling of assurance. I soon learned that I had nailed the job.

Weeks later, James and I were back in Spokane, utilizing our accrued vacation hours to look for a place to live. We drove around looking for available rentals, but found nothing. After driving across town, we stumbled upon the South Hill and loved it. On our last opportune day, James spotted a little house for rent on the main road. We called the property management company and arranged for a viewing that day. As we walked through the living room with a beautiful fireplace and bookshelves on each side, the small but modern kitchen, and the three bedrooms, we knew it was perfect for out little family of four. But when we looked out the window in the master bedroom into a big backyard, we were overjoyed. James and I had never had a yard. We had lived in apartments, duplexes, and even a tent, but we had never had a house that seemed like a permanent residence. Caught in a daydream like young newlyweds, we lay on the floor by the big window in the master bedroom and envisioned all the wonderful blessings of living in this home.

Later, we sat in the living room with the late-afternoon sunlight pouring in, and James began to dream about ministry—something he often did before each move, as if his spirit was lifted every time we took a new step on the map. We had moved a lot, and every time, James would brainstorm about ministry opportunities and his aspirations to do something big for God. But nothing ever came of these dreams. Usually the fear of not having enough money held us back. That lion was always crouching at the door, waiting to devour us.

But sitting on the hardwood floor that afternoon, he said, "Heather, can't you see it? This is a perfect place to invite a small group?"

Caught in the moment, I was hopeful, though also cautious because of the downward spirals he usually had after settling. I knew the patterns. He'd start out by going to church on a regular basis. Then he'd get frustrated by people asking him how his job search was coming along, especially during prayer requests. While everyone was always encouraging, it always felt like a big blow to his pride. Then he'd shut himself off from church, fellowship, and eventually he'd be wishing he could be a lone survivalist in the woods in northern Idaho. Finally, he'd find a job, and he'd let that take precedence over his schedule.

We rented the house and were able to move in before I started my new job. My friend Tracy helped us pack. I groaned when she arrived to help, as I did not want to leave her. She had become such a dear friend, but at least it was a soft goodbye. We would be staying in the same region.

The first year in Spokane was bliss. Jake and Lizzy got into a great school, with Lizzy starting kindergarten and Jake beginning second grade. They both loved their new school, and once James was able to quit his job at the ski resort in Sandpoint, he helped them get ready for school in the mornings. After work, I'd come home to find them all together, playing in the backyard with James.

When I talked to Tracy for the first time after our move, I said, "It all seems too good to be true." But I had this feeling that something was lurking ahead, and I shared my concern with her. She encouraged me to embrace the blessing of this rich season in our life together, which I did.

One day, I came home from work and discovered that James had rigged a zip line in the backyard, using his climbing ropes and gear. Lizzy's face lit-up as she stood high up on the tree by her dad's side, ready to fly on the line. After she overcame her initial fear, she wanted to do it again and again and again. Jake was the same.

Another time, I came home to a horrible smell. James looked at me like a teenager who just dented the car and said, "Sorry about the toaster oven." He had used it to make a sheath for his knife. The sheath came out great, but the toaster oven was kaput. Another day I came home to find James building a fire in the backyard with Jake, teaching him how to start the fire with friction.

Other times I'd come home to a boxing match. Jake and Lizzy's little hands would be covered in their dad's big boxing gloves for a rumble in the living room. James was living as I remembered him from when we first met. Throughout our years of marriage with children, he had always had to work nightshifts and weekends. Coming home to find James playing with the kids was a priceless gift.

That first year, we also connected with Real Life Ministries Spokane, a new church plant, and started attending a small group Bible study down the block. But sadly, as doubt and worry crept in, James became more and more irritated. Rather than reflecting on the goodness of this time with his family, he felt defeated about not having a job, and so he dropped out of the small group and said it was not for him. As before, I kept going without him.

Though he continued to attend church services each Sunday morning, he started to complain about having to set up the chairs in the elementary school where we met each week. As we drove down the South Hill for the service one Sunday, we hit some ice at a red light, and he said in frustration, "Let's go to that church you went to." I had been going to some evening services at Southside Christian Church a bit closer to our house, so we turned around and headed back up the hill.

As we walked into the renovated old cinema, James was moved and said that we should start going there. *Okay,* I agreed, and just like that, we were in an entire new community, making new friends again.

I have come to see that slipping on the ice was no accident—nor was stumbling onto our house on Grand Boulevard. Some call these moments *luck,* while others call them *chance,* but I call them *divine interruptions*—like a billboard telling us to turn around or go another way. If we are listening, tuned in, we will hear the words, "This is the way; walk in it."

I call [these moments] divine interruptions—like a billboard telling us to turn around or go another way. If we are listening, tuned in, we will hear the words, 'This is the way; walk in it.'

James finally did find a loss prevention job at a corporate pharmacy. Our lives returned to the same old patterns and irregular schedules. Dinners were missed and weekends were dismantled.

That summer, my parents invited the kids to drive with them across the United States in their RV, as they had with me when I was younger. James and I were relieved to get a break from the wear and tear of parenthood, as we couldn't afford the luxury of babysitters, and we're excited to get a little honeymoon.

After my parents picked up Jake and Lizzy, we followed them to the WalMart in Airway Heights and hung out in the RV for awhile to talk about all the places they would travel, going over all the points of interest on the map. Someone snapped a picture of us before they took off for their first destination in Montana. Later, looking at the photo on my screen, I noticed that James looked bigger than ever before, especially compared to his river guiding days. He also wouldn't smile. He was just grumpy—a season I'd seen so many times before. I really wanted my old James back and hoped that this time with just the two of us would be special.

We finally got our schedules worked out so that James could take a weekend off, so we wound the mountain roads to the little town of Leavenworth, a quaint Bavarian town tucked away in the Cascades. James wanted to be spontaneous and explore, so we parked off the road, scrambled across rocks, and made our way to a bridge across a river. The sky was clear and blue, the air smelled of pine trees, and the temperature was warm—a spectacular day to spend time together. We stopped to take pictures on the old railroad bridge, and he stood with his arms crossed, feet apart, his face serious. He always did this when he posed for a picture.

We held hands as we walked the flat trail parallel to the river. As we continued down the path, we came across a wooden cross that was planted in the ground, about two feet high. A laminated paper was attached, and we knelt down to read it. The story shared that years ago, a youth group had come to this section of the river, and one of them had fallen in and been swept downstream. Another went after him, and then another. Several died that day, and this was their memorial.

James sat silently on a wooden bench nearby. I was struck by how much time James was taking to sit and contemplate this story.

After the weekend, we returned to everyday life, and then James decided we should go on an overnight backpacking excursion. We hadn't backpacked in years, but we packed our bags and hit a nearby trail in Liberty Lake. It was a good hike, and we passed flowing creeks and an old, uninhabited cabin. Eventually, we set up our tent for the night. Although I had hoped for something romantic, James sat outside the tent in silence to be by himself. I didn't even get a kiss goodnight. I wondered what he was thinking about, but we woke the next day, packed our tent, and he never shared what was on his mind. James had a tendency to be mysterious in this way often throughout our marriage, but this was different.

The next Saturday morning, we were sitting on our back deck, which overlooked our backyard. As the sun rose in the brisk summer air of Spokane, we sat under a blanket, drinking coffee and talking. I longed for and loved these moments of being together at peace, when life seemed to stand still around us. My legs were folded on top of his lap as we sat, sipping from our mugs and enjoying the warmth of the sun on our faces. James had that same reflective expression he'd had while sitting by the memorial cross and later on our camping trip. He began talking about faith and a desire to do more for God. Though I had heard it all before, he was so sincere. I knew in my spirit that this was real. He truly wanted to follow the Lord. I felt goose bumps, confident that my desperate plea was finally being answered.

Our mini-honeymoon ended, and my parents returned with the children, having had some wild excursions like a great storm that shook their RV in Montana. They had seen many of the sights I had seen when I was a youth, such as Mount Rushmore and Yellowstone. My parents offered to continue the journey, taking all of us to the Oregon coast, but James didn't think he could ask for time off from his new job. Because I had the vacation accrued, I took a week to join them on the drive to Oregon.

We traversed the lush green, moss-covered Northwest, and then the landscape changed as we drew closer to the coast. Unlike the Florida and North Carolina coastlines we were familiar with in the South, the Pacific Ocean was cooler, and the waves crashed upon rocky cliffs. Our first stop was Canon Beach, a cute little town with small brown cabins and brightly colored trim along the windows. The little town opens to a beach with an incredible view of large boulders on the coast. Though the experience was rich, I was missing James. I longed for him to be with us, with his family.

When we arrived back home, James regretted not going with us. His work in loss prevention at the pharmacy was taking a toll on him and pulling him into despair. He wasn't able to meet his quota of "stops" (catching the thief in action), and he lived on coffee, soda, energy drinks, and anything that would give him a boost. This pattern certainly wasn't anything new, but when he called my parents to beg them to come back to Spokane and take another trip to Oregon, it was obvious that something was different.

With our family back together and the school year upon us, James had a burst of enthusiasm one weekend and wanted to get out of the house. He packed all our rock climbing gear, and we loaded the car to go to Minnehaha on the Spokane River. As always, James set up the top rope, as I was never comfortable setting the safety, taking Jake along to teach him. As Lizzy played, I looked up to see James instructing Jake about his many experiences in the wild, on rescues, and as a lone ranger on the trails. I grabbed my camera and took a silhouette of them together, father and son.

When they came back down, we started to climb, and James instructed Jake about the commands "belay on" and "climb on."

Jake started climbing up the wall, but he grew frustrated because he couldn't make it up off the ground for long. James explained the strategy to him, showed him where to hold on, and sometimes I worried he was pushing him a bit too hard. Finally, Jake made it past the hard maneuver. By the time he made it to the overhang, he stood proudly on top looking down at us with a big grin and arms crossed. We all cheered for him. He belayed him down, full of life and excitement. When he took off his harness, he got a high five from his dad.

Then we helped Lizzy get in the harness. Though she was just as entertained by the flowers as she was climbing the rock, she was eager to give it a try. James would touch her on the back and instruct her, as he had with Jake. Her little fingers reached for the good handholds, and she struggled just like Jake through the first section, but finally managed to get past the most difficult part. When she made it to the top, we clapped and cheered. Her climbing helmet tilted to one side as she smiled, revealing some of the teeth she had recently lost. The smile quickly faded when she realized she had to come down. The scariest part was leaning out from the rock and trusting James to belay her down, but with some reassurance and coaching, James slowly brought her to the ground.

After the climb, James went to clean up all the gear, and I took more pictures of Jake and Lizzy, who were both in high spirits. They held each other tightly and grinned. I didn't want to forget this day.

Both Jake and Lizzy shed tears of frustration on that first outdoor climbing experience, but they conquered their fears and tackled that huge, rough wall, with a little help from their dad. I could see God's handprints all over that day. He knew all that was before us and was speaking to us, guiding our every little step like a good shepherd.

God had led me to a good job in Spokane and helped us find a house. He had given James quality time with Jake and Lizzy while he was unemployed. He had guided us to do a U-turn and directed us to Southside Christian Church. He had led James and I to the river and to that old wooden cross. He had opened the door for Jake, Lizzy, and I to travel to the Oregon coast with my parents, giving me a glance at what was ahead, with an empty seat beside me. He had inspired James to take us climbing, giving us a lasting memory and showing us all how the Good Shepherd would harness and coach us up the rock face of life.

The Lord is my shepherd; I shall not want. He makes me lie down in green pastures. He leads me beside still waters. He restores my soul. He leads me in paths of righteousness for his name's sake.
—Psalm 23:1–3
New American Standard Bible

∼ 10 ∼

HIS TESTS

EVERY MORNING I would park about a ten-minute walk away from my workplace at Greater Spokane Incorporated. I loved watching the gorgeous reflection of the sunrise in the sky, and as I crossed the bridge over the Spokane River, I noticed how it surged with power in the spring and then dwindled in the fall and winter. I enjoyed the natural beauty and the city structures as I passed by City Hall, through Riverfront Park Square, and continued on to work. During that ten-minute walk, I talked to God, and for nearly a year, I heard a faint whisper, "Trust Me." One day I realized, *Yes, trust Him!* I had to trust God through all the rapids of my life, even the Broken Nose, Hell's Hole, or Grumpy's that might be lurking ahead.

Fall 2011 (Spokane, Washington)

Around the third week of September, James mentioned that he had a headache and sinus infection. He often had sinus headaches and allergies during the change of seasons, and so I didn't think much about it. As I popped a frozen pizza in the oven, he asked, "Heather, will you go with me to the doctor?"

"You'll be just fine," I said hastily. "You don't need me to go to the doctor with you."

"Please," he said.

"I just put a pizza in the over, and I need to help Jake and Lizzy with their homework," I snapped.

"Okay," he said, bowing his head, but I couldn't help seeing the disappointment on his face.

Frustrated that he wanted me to accompany him to a doctor's appointment for a sinus infection, I continued preparing dinner and shrugged it off.

The clinic said he had a sinus infection and gave him the usual medications, but his headache did not go away. Days later, I got a call at work.

"Heather, I need you to come pick me up," pleaded James. I could hear his panicked breathing in between every word.

"Where are you?" I asked.

"I'm at Jack in the Box." His voice sounded frantic.

"Which one, James? Are you close to work?" I felt anxious as I tried to figure out where he was.

"Yeah. I'm not sure how I got here," he said, "and I hit the curb on the way here."

"James, can you tell me the street you are on?" His breathing became even heavier.

"I'm on Pines," he said at last.

"Okay, I'm on my way."

I hung up the phone and began to question how I was going to tell my boss I needed to leave. *My husband doesn't know where he is, so I need to pick him up.* It made him sound crazy. I figured he was having some kind of anxiety attack. I had seen him have one years before. Despite my insecurities, I told my boss the wild truth. Concern was written all over her face as she gave me her approval. I hurried off, my mind scattered, as I wondered what was happening to James.

I worried that his loss prevention job was stressing him out. He hadn't been meeting his quota of thieves each week. *Could he be having a mental breakdown?*

After driving across town, I finally reached Pines and spotted his car in the parking lot at Jack in the Box. When he got in the car, he was a nervous wreck, so jittery and confused, his palms sweaty. We left his car in the lot, and I drove him home.

Later that afternoon, I picked up the kids from school and after dinner, we packed the kids in the Subaru to go pick up his car.

James seemed much better, but when we arrived, James said, "Heather, stay close."

"Okay, but you need to stay with me," I joked, because he always called me a "turtle" driver since I tend to be slow and cautious.

As we headed home, he stayed right behind me on the interstate and continued along our normal route. But as we began our ascent up South Hill along the curvy roads in the dark, I lost sight of his headlights tailing behind me. I kept driving, thinking that James had been stopped at a light. He was so close to home that he couldn't get lost. As we pulled into the driveway, Jake grew concerned.

Once we were inside, Jake jumped on the brown leather couch and asked, "Mom, is Dad going to be okay?"

We snuggled together while Lizzy went on to bed, as it was quite late. Jake was as worried as I was. He and James were two peas in a pod.

I went outside, needing a breath of fresh air, and called James on his cell phone, but he didn't pick up. I thought maybe his battery was down or he didn't have it with him. I went back inside and continued to wait and wait with Jake, who finally fell asleep around eleven. I went back outside. "God, where could James be?" I whispered. Just as I had prayed for my shoes when young, I was now praying to find my husband, who was lost in the darkness of the night.

After pacing back and forth down our driveway and along the sidewalk, my heart skipped a beat when I saw the familiar Subaru, but then he kept driving past our house. I ran after him, waving my arms, but he continued driving away. He kept pushing on the brakes, jarring the car, which was swerving over the yellow and white lines. My heart sank as I watched him drive away.

He was gone for another fifteen grueling minutes, but eventually he found his way home.

Panic-stricken, I yelled, "James, where have you been?" as he got out of the car.

"Heather, this place is so confusing. I took one wrong turn, and then I've been driving up and down these streets. You know how the South Hill is." His hands shook as he spoke.

Never once did he admit that something was wrong. *What was happening to my husband?* Our world was shaking, and I felt so alone. I couldn't even pray.

Over the next several days, the symptoms grew worse. One evening James woke up at one in the morning convinced that there were people coming out of the shadows in our bedroom. In my sleepy state, I kept telling him to go back to bed and assured him it was just a bad dream. For an hour, he paced back and forth, trying to persuade me that people were watching us.

"Some people like to mess with you and come into your house and move things around," he said, his eyes wide-open.

"James, honey, there is no one in our room," I told him. "Go back to bed."

"I left my machete right here, and someone moved it over here." James had many guns, knives, and other weapons. He took care of each one and kept them securely out of reach. He always knew where they were.

"James, please, no one is here."

I rolled over and tried to go back to sleep, as I felt there was nothing I could do for him.

Later, he woke me up again and told me that there were people coming out of the screen on our computer. "James, you have got to be kidding!" I felt completely exhausted.

With seriousness, he said, "No. Look. Don't you see?"

I looked at the computer. I didn't see them. I felt like my heart was being wrung out. He clearly saw the people, and there was nothing I could do to convince him otherwise. Somehow I went back to sleep.

The next morning, when my alarm went off, I found James asleep by my side. I slipped out of bed to get ready for work, and on my way to the bathroom, I tripped. In the dim, pre-dawn light, I was confused to discover the space heater cord had been tied to our bedpost. Like the many traps James had made to catch squirrels in the woods, he had booby trapped our bedroom to protect us from the people he thought were coming to get us. I stood still and wept, then unwound the knot he had tied in the cord.

Determined to find an answer before work, I searched Google for short term memory loss, headaches, hallucinations, anxiety, all James's symptoms over the last weeks. The results revealed everything from mental disorders to depression, dementia, and brain tumors.

As I got dressed, I was in a state of confusion and shock as I scrolled through our late night conversations and James's bizarre behavior.

As I walked across the bridge of the Spokane River, I prayed. *Trust Me,* God continued to whisper. I didn't know what else I could do. I knew I couldn't get lost in a frenzy of worry or our family would get pulled under the pounding waves and drown. I had to trust that we were in the palm of our loving Father's hand and He would carry us through.

> *I had to trust that we were in the palm of our loving Father's hand and He would carry us through.*

When I arrived at work, I went upstairs to see a co-worker and ended up telling her everything that had happened, trying to find order and to trust God in the chaos. She encouraged me to go home. Then I shared what had happened with my boss, who repeated the words, "Go home."

Determined to finish my work, I ignored their words. I had to get ready for a workshop—make coffee, cut pastries, and set up the computer and projector for the presentation. Once the room was ready, I started registering the participants as they trickled in. When it was time for the program to start, I stood up, welcomed everyone, and introduced the main speaker, but as I sat down in the back of the room, I knew I wasn't there mentally. I knew I needed to heed my coworkers' advice and leave.

As I drove home, distraught and completely drained, I prepared mentally for an intense conversation with James. *How would I convince him that he needed help?* Walking in the door, I asked him to sit down. He sat in the computer chair, and I sat on our bed, looking at the bedpost where the trap had been set the night before. Then I looked James in the eyes and gently explained that he needed to see a doctor again. I told him that I would be there for him this time. He nodded in agreement.

As we drove to the urgent care, James begged me not to tell the doctor what had happened the night before. Not sure if I should respect his wishes, I said with reservation, "Okay, I won't tell."

As we waited in the stark white office, I contemplated what I would say. When the doctor arrived, James became a bundle of nerves and acted as if he were being examined by a judge who was giving him a death sentence. The doctor had him stand up, take off his shirt, and do odd things like touch his nose. With each command, James shook with anxiety.

The doctor noted that he had been there before, and James explained that he still had headaches. The doctor said he needed to give the medicine more time. Then I told the doctor about the memory loss, how James had forgotten how to drive home from work, and other peculiarities, though I kept quiet about the hallucinations. He said James had probably had an anxiety attack.

"But what about him forgetting how to drive home?" I asked.

"Do you live nearby?" When I said we did, he replied, "Well, have him drive home."

I was startled by his comment, but gave James the keys so he could drive home. As soon as he pulled out of the parking lot, he said, "Heather, do I take a right turn here?" My heart sank. "Yes," I said and then continued to tell him the way home.

Then James received a letter from Jake and Lizzy's school about how frequently they were late to school. While timeliness was never his strength, it was his responsibility to take them to school each day, and though he didn't tell me about the letter until later, it triggered him to call his dad in Mississippi for help. Somehow he knew his condition was serious, but he never admitted it to me. His dad said he would book a flight to visit just as soon as he could.

After the letter, James decided to go back to the clinic for a follow-up visit while I was at work. When I came home, James told me how he had seen the same doctor, and he had threatened to notify the state that James should be sent to a mental institution. This wrong presumption further escalated James's anxiety and pushed him towards a mental breakdown.

James had been poked and prodded most of his childhood as he battled leukemia, but he rarely talked about it. After this experience at the urgent care clinic, I pleaded with James to call St. Jude's Hospital in Memphis, where he had been treated as a child, and ask them for an opinion about his symptoms. Two years earlier, he had taken part in a research study with others who had been treated for leukemia, and he had discovered that the radiation to his brain had caused many of the cognitive issues that had challenged him over the years. He had been invited to participate in another study that November related to memory loss. Feeling certain that they might have some answers, I begged him to call. He finally gave in, but he asked me to make the call.

I phoned with great hope that someone would be able to help James. A nurse in the research division answered the phone. I introduced myself and explained that James had been invited to participate in research on memory loss and how recently, James had been experiencing memory loss, anxiety, headaches, and confusion.

Without hesitation, she said, "You need to get him in immediately for a CAT scan. You can't wait until November for him to come to Memphis." I took a breath as I hung up, knowing how difficult it would be to convince James that he needed to go for further examination.

Later, I cried as I told James about the conversation, but he stoically agreed. Before we left for a different clinic, I jotted down all the symptoms I had observed and slipped the paper in my pocket, knowing I would need to give it to the doctor secretively. I resolved not to go to another doctor just to be turned away without a thorough investigation.

We arrived just before the offices closed, and as we checked in, I slid the piece of paper to the receptionist and asked her to look it over as I filled out the paperwork. She opened it, her face registering a brief look of shock, and then excused herself.

Before long, we were called into a small room, and I silently wondered if this would end up like all the other doctor visits.

The doctor arrived and asked James about his headaches, pointing to his forehead and then the back of his neck. James told the same story about his sinus infections. The doctor said that where James was pointing did not indicate a sinus infection, and so he would like to do a CAT scan, but the lab was closed for the day. He asked us to come back early the next day.

The next day, a woman asked us a lot of questions and took some blood to rule out a vitamin deficiency. We shared what had transpired and the recommendation we had received from the nurse at St. Jude's. After a careful examination, she scheduled a CAT scan and said she would see us again to discuss the results.

I waited anxiously in the lobby while James was escorted to the CAT scan. I knew how much James hated tests. After the scan, we headed back to the second floor and waited until we were called back to review the results. The nurse paused as she looked at us, and then with tears in her eyes, she said, "I am so sorry... you have a tumor."

James clasped his hands, smiled, and said, "Thank you for telling me with such compassion." We were both grateful at that moment just to have an answer. Then James broke the intense moment and said, "At least I'm not crazy." We all laughed.

James handled the news as if he were facing a high-stress emergency evacuation or river rescue—with peace and a readiness to act. I was grateful for his steadiness and positive attitude.

After exiting the office, James thanked every doctor and nurse along the way. As we were leaving the clinic, James' dad phoned to say that he had arrived at the airport. James told him to get a cab, as we needed to go get the kids from school and then head back to the clinic.

James Earl arrived in the taxi just before we had to leave to pick up Jake and Lizzy. We welcomed him with hugs and briefly shared the results about the tumor. He was unflustered and sturdy, which was exactly what we needed in that moment.

We all headed to the school together, which was only a few blocks from our house. Jake and Lizzy were elated to see their granddaddy for this unexpected visit, as they rarely got to see him because of the distance between us. We hadn't known when he would be able to arrive and were amazed at his miraculous timing. After hugs and chatter, they hopped in the back seat, and we went back to the clinic. Full of excitement, Jake and Lizzy told their granddaddy every detail about their day and then asked why he had come. When we explained a little bit about the tumor, my heart broke, and I wondered, *How will they handle what's happening to their daddy?*

At the clinic, we all went together to review the scans. We wanted to stick together as a family and to give Jake and Lizzy as much information as possible so their minds wouldn't fill in the blanks with false information. As we stared at the black and white pictures of James' brain, we could see a mass right in the middle. Everyone barraged the nurse with questions about the mass and how to get rid of it. She answered graciously and assured us she would find the best doctors to help us take the next steps.

We headed home with more questions than answers, then stopped at a grocery store to pick up food for dinner. As we walked around the store, James put his arm around my shoulders and whispered, "Heather, I feel like life is slipping away." Resting my head on his shoulder and clinging to his hand, I cried. I didn't want to let him go.

That night, James asked his dad and me to pray with him. He got on his knees in our bedroom and prayed for God to forgive him for the pornography he'd been looking at since a boy and throughout our marriage. He also shared other sins that were heavy on his heart and asked for forgiveness. After his confession, he told his dad where he had hidden the pornography in the basement. Then he asked me to start writing his will. I had always been his scribe for cover letters and resumes, but now I was transcribing instructions about what to do if he were to die. He only had a few requests—including that he not be put on a machine to keep him alive. He wanted quality of life over a quantity of days.

A few days later, as James Earl, James, and I were sitting around the table enjoying lunch, James unexpectedly asked, "Heather, do you think James Earl is a man of good character?"

"Yes, of course," I replied.

James then said that he wanted me to remarry again because I would need a husband. He said that any man I was interested in should meet James Earl for approval. He said it without a tear or regret, but I couldn't fathom anyone other than James.

Though we were in a fog of darkness, faint glimmers of God's presence shone around us—through the nurse's gentleness and compassion, James Earl's arrival at the perfect moment, being together as we reviewed the scans, James's moving confession as he surrendered to Jesus, and the peace that flooded me in the following days, which truly surpassed all understanding. I was learning to trust God with our lives as we braced ourselves to enter this tumultuous rapid. Though our family was riding a small boat through some towering, raging waves, we did not need to be afraid, because Jesus was right there with us in the boat.

I wanted to lean into the challenges ahead of us and rely on the power of Jesus to carry us through those surging waves, just as I had learned during my river guiding days to rely on the power of the water rather than my own strength. James had taught me that, and I wanted to count the trials we were facing as joy, knowing that "the testing of . . . faith produces steadfastness" (James 1:2–3).

In this you rejoice, though now for a little while, if necessary, you have been grieved by various trials, so that the tested genuineness of your faith—more precious than gold that perishes though it is tested by fire—may be found to result in praise and glory and honor at the revelation of Jesus Christ.
–1 Peter 1:6–7
New American Standard Bible

~ 11 ~

HIS HEART

NOW THAT WE knew that James had cancer, we couldn't just float through our days together as if we were in a calm backwater, or try to paddle futilely backwards against the raging current of his disease, or try to skirt the painful rapid to avoid it. We had to keep paddling forward—just as James had taught me to ride through Hell's Hole on the Ocoee River by keeping the nose of my boat pointed straight into the rapid to avoid flipping. The only command was, "ALL FORWARD!" We just had to paddle on as hard as we could, trusting our lives to God's perfect will.

September 2011 (Spokane, Washington)

James, James Earl, Jake, Lizzy and I all went to meet James's neurosurgeon in his office, which was filled with molds and pictures of brains. A large medieval painting of a group of men dissecting a brain hung above his desk. Plaques and framed degrees covered the wall. The doctor had hair as blond as Barbie's Ken and looked about the same age as James, thirty-nine years old. As we sat before him in nice leather chairs, he assured us of his credentials and explained in scientific jargon what the mass could be.

Like a student ready at the front of the class, I conscientiously took down everything he said on a yellow note pad, scribbling notes in layman's terms: not cancerous, cancerous, or seriously cancerous.

The doctor showed us the MRI and explained that the tumor was in the middle of James's brain and was roughly the size of a golf ball. At the time, I didn't understand what a tumor that size meant for James, but I came to understand as I witnessed the ongoing deterioration of his brain. As the doctor explained how he'd extract the tissue out of James's brain, he compared himself to a mechanic to help us understand his role in the team of doctors who would be treating James. He said he would be the first doctor to enter the "match," and then another doctor would step in, and eventually he would step out all together as the other doctors made new plays.

The children had heard the word *cancer* from the stories James had told them about his childhood fight with leukemia, but as we listened to the doctor, I wondered how they were processing all the information and worried about their fears. *Oh, this is too much.*

After scheduling a biopsy, we left the doctor's office, passing one brain model after another on our way to the exit. I felt perplexed and overwhelmed.

When we arrived home, James and I sat down with the children and said we wanted to be open and honest about what was happening with their dad. We invited them to be a part of the doctor visits when possible.

"Could daddy die?" Jake asked.

"Yes," we said.

After a pause, Jake asked, "Can I go play football?"

Over the next several weeks, Jake and Lizzy seemed distracted by having their granddaddy in town, and they started to shy away from James as his health declined and strange things began to happen.

One evening, we were having dinner with a friend in our living room, and James dropped his plate full of food. When it smashed on the floor, James didn't react or bend over to pick up all the broken pieces, and so I knelt on the floor to clean it up. At the time, I was puzzled, but I didn't know then that in the months ahead, I would have to feed James when he could no longer hold a fork.

Another evening, I heard, *Bam!* and when I ran to see what had happened, I found James on the floor of our small shower. As I helped him back up to his feet, I didn't know that in the days ahead, he would fall more and more frequently.

As James grew weaker on his left side, he struggled to walk and had to wrap his arm around me for support. I was grateful to have James Earl living with us, as he helped me bear a lot of the physical weight of caring for James.

For most of our marriage, James and I had lived paycheck to paycheck, but we had always tried to keep a $1,000 emergency fund, though that had dwindled down to $300. As James' health declined, he had to quit his job, and we were trying to cover all our living and medical expenses on my income and the cheap temporary health insurance plan we had purchased while he was unemployed. We knew that we could end up bankrupt, but as we sat in the living room one afternoon, discussing our finances, James said, "Heather, I have complete peace about this." This was not a typical response for James, as he worried a lot about our finances, but I knew he believed what he was saying, and I had complete peace, too.

That evening, we went to a service at Southside Christian Church. At the end of the service, during the announcements, James leaned over and said, "I think we should do this Bible study class." He had never expressed a desire to read or study the Bible, and so I was excited, but also cautiously pessimistic.

"Really?" I asked. "Are you serious?"

We attended the Bible study class that next week and ended up sitting in the front, since we arrived late and all the other seats were filled. Pastor Rob shared about missionaries serving abroad who were "devouring the Word of God." James stopped Pastor Rob in the middle of his teaching and asked, "How is it that I could believe in Jesus my whole life but never have a desire for God's Word?"

Pastor Rob smiled at James and then gazed at me.

"Is this your wife?" he asked.

"Yes," James replied.

"How did you pursue her?" he asked. "Did you get to know all about her and spend time with her?" James nodded. "Did you like the things she liked?" Pastor Rob described how a relationship with God is similar, and God pursues us in a love relationship through Jesus. Just as James sought me, James needed to seek God and build a relationship with Him by reading His Word and talking with Him and loving what He loves and doing what He says.

Then James announced that he had a brain tumor. Pastor Rob said, "Let's take a moment and pray for James." After praying, the class took a short break, and people started coming up to James, encouraging him to read God's Word. I felt like I was witnessing prayers being answered—most especially mine!

We had to leave the class early to pick up our children, and while I was trying to sneak out, James turned to the class, lifted his hands in complete surrender, and shouted, "I LOVE JESUS!" The class cheered.

I blushed, but felt awed by the work God was doing inside James. *Oh, that we would all cry out His most wonderful name in front of everyone!* I thought of Matthew 10:32: "whoever acknowledges Jesus before men, He will also acknowledge him before His Father in heaven."

From that moment on, James began to grow rapidly in his faith. He no longer made excuses about going to church, and I no longer had to remind him to wait to eat until we gave God thanks. He no longer yelled at me for going to a small group to study the Word.

At a church service a few weeks later, he raised his hands throughout all the praise music, and during the sermon, which was about the Lord's prayer, both of us heard loud and clear, "Your kingdom come. *Your will be done.*" I knew that God was using this trial to bring people into His kingdom, and I knew that His will was being done. Though James was sick, I felt complete peace. I was coming to understand that James was finally living, because to live is Christ (Philippians 1:21a).

I noticed that James was becoming softer, more humble, and extremely patient. I also noticed how he treated every nurse and doctor with kindness and gratitude, even the nurses he passed in hallways.

Lizzy noticed the change in James, too. One night, while tucking her into bed, she said, "Mommy, this tumor is making daddy kinder." Then she had an epiphany. With a sparkle in her eye, she said, "The brain is not the most important part of the body. It's the heart."

"The brain is not the most important part of the body. It's the heart."

I marveled at how God was teaching Lizzy at the age of six. When I tucked her in each night, wisdom just poured out of her little lips. As she witnessed her dad's body deteriorating, God was teaching all of us what was most important.

The lyrics from the song "Blessings" by Laura Story became engraved on my soul during that season: "blessings come through raindrops… healing comes through tears." These words carried me through, comforting my soul through "sleepless nights" and "trials of this life," His "mercies in disguise."

I was reminded of a homeless man I had met in high school, who shared with me after receiving food: "It's like the heavens opened up, and God is pouring down blessings." That's exactly how I felt as I watched God work through the hands and hearts of the family and friends who surrounded us, displaying His incredible generosity and love.

The leader of my women's small group Bible study, Katherine, pulled our group together to pray for us in our home shortly after she learned that James was ill. As we sat in our living room with the warm light bursting through the old vintage windows, James and I sensed the presence of God and were touched and moved by their prayers.

Later that day, one of the ladies sent me a text, saying that she could see a light coming from James. I sensed that God was drawing James home and treasured this insight in my heart.

I remembered how James had envisioned our living room as a place for hosting a small group and realized that his desire was being fulfilled. While we had never started a small group together, this group had gathered in our living room to pray and to comfort our family—and many others would flood into our home over the next months.

Katherine insisted that we have meals delivered by friends in the church, though I had to take a step of humility to ask for help since we had always been so independent. But through her encouragement, I gave in, and people I'd never met from our church began to deliver delicious homemade meals, along with compassion and love. My co-workers also visited us and delivered meals.

Pastor Rob began to visit us every Wednesday, and he'd sit in the living room, listening to us share the latest news, then sharing a passage of Scripture. Sometimes he'd bring a loaf of bread made by his wife, Linda, which was always gone by dinner. We always cherished those visits.

One night we opened the door to find all our elders on our porch, full of smiles, giving us all hugs. James was in a wheelchair at that point, so we pushed him into the center of the room, and they surrounded him and sang hymns, filling our house with praise that brought us all to the gates of heaven, the very presence of God, and flooded our tiny home with love.

After singing, the elders placed their hands upon James and prayed for his healing as I sat as his feet, crying. After the prayer time, James shared that healing would be great, but the *ultimate* healing would be to go home to be with Jesus.

My father-in-law was deeply touched by what he called our "prayer groups." He kept saying that when he returned to Mississippi, he'd have to start one. Every morning, James Earl would go to *the man cave,* the name I gave our basement because James liked to escape there and tinker with his gear, to read the book of Romans. As we met in our kitchen for a cup of coffee each morning, James Earl would ask me difficult questions about faith and the mysteries of God's will. He asked, "Why would God allow someone like me to grow up in a Christian home but allow others to go to hell who didn't have the same privilege?" He was wrestling with some heavy theological questions.

We never asked anyone to come, and we never asked for money, but a stream of both arrived. Mail came from all across the United States, and the generous provision from families we knew as well as strangers was a miracle! I will be forever grateful for those who gave us both monetary gifts as well as gift cards. Their generosity was beyond our wildest imagination.

I began to talk more often to my friend Monica from the Marriott in Colorado. She had lost her dad to brain cancer when she was only eight years old, and her mother had raised her and six other children on her own. She had recently learned that her mother was dying, and so we were going through similar circumstances. Monica shared how her mom had shown resilience and strength after losing her husband, how she had never remarried, never taken a dime of welfare, and worked hard in a school cafeteria to raise her children. When she said that her mom was always on her knees in prayer, I knew that I wanted to be that kind of woman, too.

As James returned to Jesus with his whole heart, God's love poured in from the east and west and the north and south through the presence of those who visited, warm meals that filled our bellies, shoulders to cry on, ears to listen, and prayerful intercession when I could not even pray a word. As Christ began to "dwell" in our "hearts through faith," James and I became more "rooted and grounded in love," and we had the "strength to comprehend... the breadth and length and height and depth" of "the love of Christ that surpasses knowledge" as we were "filled with all the fullness of God" (Ephesians 3:17–19).

I will give them a heart to know that I am the Lord,
and they shall be my people and I will be their God, for
they shall return to me with their whole heart.
—Jeremiah 24:7
New American Standard Bible

~ 12 ~

His Food

I N THE OUTDOORS, it's imperative to pack light, but on multi-day trips on the river, the last thing you want to pack light on is food, since guides and customers become ravenous after being in the sun and paddling hard all day. James always had granola bars tucked in his many survival and first aid kits, but this crisis required something lasting. As his body began to weaken, his appetite for the truth grew, and James began to turn to the timeless book that he had heard as a boy. As he was nourished with words of everlasting life, his inner man was strengthened. The man who stood with such calm and poise in crisis on the banks of the river was now physically weakening, but he was trusting God to sustain him.

October—November 2011 (Spokane, Washington)

Just like the missionaries that Pastor Rob told us about who devoured the Word of God, James's hunger for the Word increased more and more. Every day he'd ask me to read the Scriptures to him, and then he would digest the passage and begin to ask questions. I marveled as he became all-consumed with learning more about God. We continued going to church together, and we held one another tightly as we sang songs of praise together. Eventually, as James grew weaker, we had to stop attending Pastor Rob's Bible class, but James stayed committed to learning and growing in faith.

His appetite for food increased after he began taking steroids to reduce the swelling of the tumor—beef tips, cheeseburgers, and especially homemade lasagna. James's appetite for homemade lasagna was sparked when Michaela, the mother of one of Lizzy's friends, invited James and I for dinner one night. She had just moved to a new apartment and couldn't wait to have us over. She cooked a delicious lasagna meal, which we ate slowly as we talked around her dining room table. After eating a full plate, James asked for more. I blushed, but Michaela enthusiastically went back to the kitchen to prepare a second plate. When she returned, she cheerfully said that James could eat as much as he wanted. After finishing that second plate, Michaela prepared him a third, and she and I watched in amazement as he continued to eat. Like a little boy, he kept looking up to her, batting his eyes, saying, "Please, more?" Thankfully, Michaela had a sense of humor, and as a nurse, she understood the impact of the steroids. Even still, our jaws dropped as we saw him completely devour the feast she had prepared. Over the weeks and months ahead, Michaela continued bringing us lasagnas, and James gladly ate all of them.

In early October, my older sister, Tara, offered to come out for a few days. It meant so much that she was willing to drop everything, and I realized that I needed her.

It was her first visit to the Northwest, as she was a busy mom with a full-time job, husband, and two children. Because it was her first time in the Northwest, I wanted to show her a warm welcome, give her a tour, and a mini-vacation. Though I knew her visit was not meant to be a vacation, nor a time for exploration, I had lost hold of reality. But Tara knew from what I had told her that these few days might be her last with James.

Excited, I picked her up at her hotel along with James, Jake, and Lizzy, and said that we could either drive around the city or make a day trip to Sandpoint. But before we were a block away, James was hungry, and so we stopped at a nearby Jack in the Box. We helped James out of the car and situated him at a table while we went to order. When we arrived with our trays full of food, we distributed everything, and after a blessing, James leaned over and began to eat Tara's food. Puzzled, we all looked at each other and began to laugh. James had a hamburger, fries, and soda right in front of him, but he just kept eating Tara's lunch. When Tara tried to eat the lunch that was in front of James, he stole it back. My sister was caught in a pickle, as my mom would say. We all kept snickering as Tara kept trying to sneak a little something away from James.

After the meal, we tried to help James up from the chair, but he wouldn't budge. It wasn't that he didn't want to move, but more like his brain was just shut off. *System overload!* I tried to pull him up under his arms as I had learned in my college Wilderness First Responder class, but James was too heavy. Then Tara and I tried together, but to no avail, so I retrieved his wheelchair from the car, but Tara and I still couldn't transfer him.

Seeing that we were having difficulty, two men came over to help. With one on each side, they lifted him into the wheelchair, pushed him out to the car, and then cautiously maneuvered him into the passenger seat of our Subaru sedan, ensuring that he didn't hit his head. James was positioned awkwardly in the seat, his arms and legs straight and stiff, and so I adjusted each leg to fit him in as he looked at me in bewilderment, with huge eyes. Our next step was the ER, as he was having what I later learned was a seizure.

In the end, my sister's grand tour of Spokane was a Days Inn with an indoor swimming pool, a Jack in the Box, and the Deaconess ER. But her visit far surpassed any vacation packed with tourist souvenirs or Facebook photo feeds. She brought laughter, strength, comfort, and compassion, and she took home the memories of those few days with us. There was certainly never a dull moment during our time together, which was a mix of both saltiness and sweetness.

After Tara left, James had his biopsy, and we had to wake up at the crack of dawn to get him checked in. I quickly got him dressed, hurried him to the car, and then scurried to get to the hospital on time. When he insisted that he could walk by himself, I dropped him off at the nearest entrance, but I was concerned as I sat and watched him climb the stairs to the entrance. I realized that I would need to begin thinking for James and making every little decision for him, which was difficult to balance with respecting his wishes.

After parking the car, I met him in the lobby, where we sat and held hands. The room was quiet, though the early morning news rambled off the events of the day. I felt apathetic about world events, as I was in the middle of my own battlefield.

When James's name was called, we approached the desk, and as we listened to the nurse, his pants fell to his feet. I quickly stooped down to pull them up, but James simply lifted his eyebrows and gave me a funny look, as if he were thinking, *Now that was embarrassing.*

Normally, James would've completely lost it, getting frantic and blaming me for not dressing him properly, but that reality was fading out as the strong man I had known was becoming really weak. Though I felt like crying, what I needed at that moment was a little humor to help me let go and trust that everything was in God's hands. From that day forward, I never forgot his belt as I dressed him.

As we worked through the paperwork, jittery after our mortifying first impression, the nurse asked if we had insurance. We only had temporary insurance with terrible deductibles and co-pays, and I was terrified about what this biopsy would cost us, but I tried to hold fast to peace.

As we proceeded to the waiting room upstairs, where I would wait alone, I felt cold, and sorrow weighed heavily upon me. Though I had a Bible, I couldn't read it. I fidgeted, tried to pray, wrote in my prayer journal, but felt antsy until someone finally said, "Heather."

I looked up, and the nurse led me to the room where James was being prepped for the surgery. His hair was shaved, and they had drawn little small green circles on his head with a Sharpie. He had a goofy grin on his face, as he had on our wedding day, and was wrapped in the hospital's warm, white linens, as if covered in grace. He looked confident and courageous, and though I'm sure he was nervous, he was never one to show any trepidation. He had that same cool, calm manner that he had displayed time and time again on the river, on ice, and when climbing a steep rock face.

After the anesthesiologist administered the drugs, it was time for me to wait in another silent waiting room with mint-colored walls. All the people in the room were waiting anxiously for "the news." *Is it cancer? Is it terminal? How much time is left?* I tried to pray and read the Bible, but I still couldn't focus as I sat in the deadly quiet avalanche of unknowns.

When I went into the hallway to get some air, I was overjoyed to see Michaela, who had just gotten off her nightshift as a home nurse. I debriefed her about what I knew, surrounded by the vintage pictures of nurses with solemn faces that lined the hallway. Then Tracy from Sandpoint and her son, Aidan, arrived and greeted me with a big, long hug. Then James Earl arrived after dropping Jake and Lizzy off at school, and I was suddenly surrounded by loved ones who had come to be present to me at this critical moment.

Finally, the surgeon approached our circle, and as I tried to read his face, he started explaining what he had found with scientific lingo. Though he had explained the possibilities quite thoroughly in our previous doctor's appointment, I knew everyone else would be puzzled about what he was sharing. Then Michaela spoke up, "What does all this mean?" Soon everyone understood that James had the worst possible prognosis— *glioblastoma multiforme,* a highly cancerous melanoma that would require both radiation and chemotherapy. Surgery was not possible because of the risk of paralysis. Moreover, the tumor couldn't really be removed, because it would just start growing again, and if they tried to remove it completely, they would have to cut away part of his brain. The doctor estimated that he might have a year and a half to live, if that.

In shock, I needed to get away, and so James Earl, Tracy, Aiden, and I went to the cafeteria, and Michaela went home to sleep. As we talked, we distracted ourselves momentarily from all that we would have to face in the months ahead.

Finally, we could visit James in the ICU, and I knew that he was feeling better when his appetite returned. They fed him beef tips, and over the next weeks and months, wherever we went, he asked for them. I can't imagine any hospital food being that tasty, but he loved that meal. After begging the nurse for a second helping of dinner, which wasn't allowed, James asked me to run to the nearest fast-food restaurant for a cheeseburger, and so I went on a midnight prowl, looking for a cheeseburger to sneak back into the hospital. His appetite could not be stopped!

Once James was released from the hospital, Jake and Lizzy were glad to have their daddy home, since they hadn't been allowed to visit him in the ICU. It was a difficult place to be, and so I'm grateful they didn't see him there.

Early that fall, James' mother, Anita, was finally able to take family leave from the bank where she worked in Mississippi to come stay with us and help care for James.

Her flight arrived near midnight, and I had to pick her up at the airport after an exhausting day. I was quite edgy and nervous, as she had taken care of James through cancer, buried her other son, and was coming to care for James through cancer again. Before leaving for the airport, I made a pot of coffee for the road, which I drank as I sat in the car, waiting for her arrival.

Suddenly, I was desperate to go to the bathroom, but the doors into the airport were all locked. Her flight was due any minute, and there was no bathroom in sight, so I held on and waited.

When she finally arrived, we embraced one another and cried, but I was about to explode from the coffee, so I explained my situation and said that I needed to stop by a fast-food restaurant on the way home. But as we drove through downtown, many lights were off, and one place after another was locked up for the night. I walked to another restaurant next door, where a janitor was mopping the floors, and knocked on the glass door. I waved frantically and begged to use the bathroom, but he pointed at his watch and sternly shook his head. In that moment, I lost it, and as I felt the warmth run down my legs, I felt completely humiliated. Standing in front of my mother-in-law, I had wet my pants.

She was gracious and tried to help me laugh, but I was completely soaked in my own urine and had lost any sense of dignity. As I drove home, I got my seat wet and felt completely embarrassed.

As I entered our house, I tried to walk swiftly past my father-in-law without him noticing. In the bedroom, I found James lying on the bed, awake. I explained what had happened, then shamefully changed my pants and cleaned up in our bathroom. With a chuckle, James said, "Join the club!" His words completely shifted my mood. We looked at each other and laughed. He had already begun losing control of his bodily functions, as I had already changed his pants after an accident many times. It felt like we were growing old together in our thirties, and after my own accident, I could empathize with his loss of dignity. Suddenly, I felt I understood what he felt but couldn't express.

As James's health continued to deteriorate, Anita cared for him just as she had when he was a little boy. We'd take turns feeding him, putting on his shoes, cleaning his face, or brushing his teeth. It was awkward, but we both needed time with James.

Yet we had moments of laughter among all the tears, and James's increasing appetite continued to be a hot topic around our full dinner table.

One day Michaela called with a surprise. She had hired a photographer to take photos of our family. Just like our wedding day, we were surrounded by autumn leaves. Because I was the family photographer, we had few pictures of all four of us and even fewer with James's parents. On a beautiful fall day, we went to a park close to our home and gathered near a duck pond. With some of the poses, I had to help James arrange his limbs as he sat on the ground, and we had to hold him up, but we were all together, and I was overjoyed.

Michaela later brought each of us a hand-stitched quilt that she had decorated with my favorite Bible verses and images from that day. I was in awe of her gift, and it made me realize how God had tenderly sewn all the little broken pieces together. Up close, our lives seemed blurry and chaotic, but stepping back, I could see a beautiful blanket that had both light and dark colors. The patches had been sewn in tears and laughter, but we would be able to warm ourselves with those memory quilts on the cold winter days that were to come. With each little stitch, He added a bit more faith, a tinge more perseverance, a lot of character, and LOVE.

> *The patches had been sewn in tears and laughter, but we would be able to warm ourselves with those memory quilts on the cold winter days that were to come.*

The blessings continued to come, as my parents arrived in their RV and settled near so that they could help as needed. We had all four of our parents for Thanksgiving and enjoyed a grand feast together in our little living room. When we went around the table, thanking God for our blessings, Lizzy said, "Having all my grandparents here." We were all grateful to be surrounded by the people who loved us most. As we went around the table, expressing our gratitude, we shed many tears. James continued to have an incredible appetite, but I knew that something much deeper was happening within him. Like a newborn infant, he was longing for the pure spiritual milk of God's Word, and as he drank it and tasted the Lord's goodness, he was growing up into salvation (1 Peter 2:2–3). Later, I learned that *El Shaddai,* which is a Hebrew name for God Almighty in the Old Testament, literally means "breast" *(shad)* and "enough" or "sufficient" *(dai).* Though James's body was becoming weaker, El Shaddai was pouring into him the pure milk of His Word, strengthening, nourishing, and sustaining his inner man.

O taste and see that the Lord is good;
How blessed is the man who takes refuge in Him!
-Psalm 34:8
New American Standard Bible

~ 13 ~

HIS ENDURANCE

A NYONE WHO IS planning to be a river guide must train and condition. It would be foolish to jump into the river with a paddle and raft if you've never learned how to read water, swim rapids, flip the boat, or maneuver into an eddy. Any experienced guide will tell you that you need to be prepared to be underwater for extended periods of time and that bruises, cuts and pain are a part of the job description.

November–December 2011 (Spokane, Washington)

Endurance has never been my strength. In high school I said to my classmates that I would never be a runner because I didn't understand why anyone would want to torture herself by pounding on hard pavement, gasping for air, and then suffering the aftermath of cramps and shin splints. But after birthing two children, I was growing in all the wrong places and needed to lose weight.

So I started running—and I kept running. I ran on the hard pavement in Tennessee, through ice and snow in Idaho, and then over potholed streets and cracked sidewalks in Spokane, where I began to feel that I was in training for a marathon.

After hearing the word "tumor" in the doctor's office, my natural response was to go for a run. With every stride, I could feel physical pain as I breathed harder and my legs grew weaker, but I was simultaneously shedding the inner pain that had coursed so suddenly into our lives. As I cried, the tears mixed with my salty sweat and dripped into my mouth, and I tried to let go of my frustrations about the havoc and destruction in our lives. As I fled from all the demons that seemed to be chasing me and trying to tackle me, I was able to think more clearly, pray, and remember that I was alive and breathing. *Inhale. Exhale. Inhale. Exhale.*

Just as I sought to steady my pace and control my footing with each run, I tried to take control of our family's situation by taking notes at every doctor's appointment, writing as fervently as I had in my college classes in order to communicate with doctors, pharmacists, and nurses, and I needed to research James's disease to help me make decisions when no doctor or nurse was present. I followed websites on brain cancer and organized all my findings in a binder, along with a calendar of appointments, contacts, and business cards, explanations of benefits, health bills with corresponding payment receipts, and other important documents. I became my husband's personal health care administrator and nurse, keeping track of daily dosages for more than fifteen various medications that had to be given at certain times each day. I recorded the dates and times for everything related to his bodily functions—bowel movements, urine, shortness of breath, headaches, back pain, vomiting, seizures, and on and on. With so many symptoms, I recorded all the checklists on a computer spreadsheet and also kept a written diary of the day's activities. Each day felt like a thousand all rolled into one.

As I investigated his bodily malfunctions, I tried to understand *why* his hands were shaking or his vision was altered. My folders were obsessively organized, and every document was exactly where it needed to be so that I could pull it out in an emergency. I didn't want to do anything that might lead to his death.

But in spite of all my research and organization, seizures continued to send us to the ER one weekend after another. When his body stiffened, nurses would have to extract him from the car. In a room swarming with nurses who didn't understand the details of his complex disease and didn't have access to the myriad conversations I'd had with his doctors, I was his only advocate. Regardless of how many times we visited the ER, I had to go through the same questions, explaining my husband's illness and the medications he had received that day.

Time and time again, as I sat by the hospital bed, listening to the heart monitor beep, I knew that our future was completely out of my control. Though I tried to organize everything and understand what was happening to James (as if by knowing more I could somehow find a cure), his life was out of my hands.

In addition to the seizures, James suffered from chronic constipation that left him curled up in pain in bed. One night, his mom, Anita, suggested a hot bath as a good remedy to relieve the pain. But in our older house, we had to finagle James through a narrow hallway, and then the bathroom doorframe was too small for his wheelchair. So we undressed him in the hallway, and then his dad and I struggled to lift him (he weighed 170 pounds and didn't have the strength to help us), carried him a few feet, and then maneuvered him awkwardly into the tub. Just as he was safely in the bath, he became stiff as a board—another seizure. James Earl and I looked at each other, not knowing what to do, but then we somehow mustered enough strength to lift him out of the tub and get him back in the wheelchair. His body was so rigid that he felt like a life-sized nutcracker. After wheeling him back into our bedroom and lifting him into bed, James Earl and I were exhausted.

When the constipation returned, we didn't try to put him in the bath again, but it got so bad that a nurse had to come and extract James's stool by hand. As I watched James writhe in agony, I desperately wanted his suffering and pain to be over. The symptoms were mostly side-effects from the many drugs he had to ingest each day— pills that I had to force down his throat.

Another time, a nurse had to insert a catheter, and my heart wrenched as James gasped and bulged out his eyes. From then on, I then had to check his urine bag for any blood and clean out the bag and the insertion each day. I remembered my wedding vow of "in sickness and in health," and though I certainly hadn't envisioned what this might look like on my wedding day, it was now a joy to be by his side every moment, though it was agonizing to watch him suffer.

Sleeping in bed with James each night was like going to bed with an infant. Throughout the night, I would listen for his breathing to make sure he was still alive. I'd wake up automatically at around 3 a.m. for his early morning vomit, the bucket close to my bedside so that I could quickly catch it. After he threw up, I would run hot water over a wash rag, wipe off his face, and then clean up the mess. As I washed him, he'd say,

"What happened?" or talk as if nothing happened. He was rapidly losing his short-term memory.

Some mornings at around 5 a.m., I'd meet my friend Sandra to go for a run. One morning, when I was about to go, James threw up. As I was cleaning up, James Earl came in, knowing that it was time for my run. He encouraged me to run and let him take care of the rest. I was so grateful to have the help, and I really cherished those runs with Sandra. As soon as I got outside in the cold air, I felt alive. I always met Sandra with lots on my mind and often would talk the entire hour or so of our run about the intensity of the sickness and the daily drama in our home. Those runs were like therapy sessions.

The marathon with James was demanding and exhausting, and as I picked James up after he fell in the shower, held his hand when he blanked in a seizure, held his plate and fed him, brushed his teeth each morning, I often had tears in the corner of my eyes. I tried to understand him when no words came and his facial expressions were void. I fed him pills almost every hour and then later found them hidden away in his mouth. Meanwhile, I tried to keep being a mom to our two children, who were completely bewildered by how our lives had been flipped upside down. Through it all, I desperately wanted to know Jesus and His power to heal the sick and raise life from the dead. I was learning that to know His power and resurrection, I had to fellowship in His sufferings, being conformed to His death (Philippians 3:10–11).

The race was relentless, but we were not alone! God, our strength, was sustaining us.

The race was relentless, but we were not alone. God, our strength, was sustaining us. Even though we had no words to pray sometimes, the Holy Spirit cried and groaned words for us that were too deep for our understanding. As we lived through the dark valley of sickness and faced James's death, we were carried in the hands of the One who had made us.

Like my first 10K run at Bloomsday in Spokane, we were surrounded by people who encouraged us to continue running the race of life. People gave us water bottles that quenched our thirst whenever they offered prayers, meals, gifts, listening ears, or hugs. The doctors, nurses, and office clerks in the hospitals and clinics uplifted us with their constant high-fives. So many people spurred us on so that we could make it to the finish line with our eyes fixed on Jesus, the Forerunner, who had already gone before us and endured the suffering of the cross. By looking at Jesus, I could run with hope rather than growing weary or losing heart. As I came to know Him more and to understand his suffering and the power of His resurrection more fully, I knew that He was teaching me forbearance, endurance, and patience through James, even though he was confined to a wheelchair and had only a few months to live.

Therefore, since we have so great a cloud of witnesses surrounding us, let us also lay aside every encumbrance and the sin which so easily entangles us, and let us run with endurance the race that is set before us, fixing our eyes on Jesus, the author and perfecter of faith, who for the joy set before Him endured the cross, despising the shame, and has sat down at the right hand of the throne of God. For consider Him who has endured such hostility by sinners against Himself, so that you may not grow weary and lose heart.
—Hebrews 12:1–3
New American Standard Bible

~ 14 ~

HIS SILENCE

J ust before going over a waterfall, there is a short time of quiet when you can't hear the sound of what's ahead of you. Then *bam*, your boat is tipping over the falls, and you can hear the waves crashing violently against the rocks. Along the river there are also long, drawn out times of silence between one rapid to another. In the same way, there are times when God seems to take His people through seasons of silence, such as the four hundred years between the Old Testament to the New Testament before Jesus Christ came from heaven to earth, fulfilling God's promises as He spoke to the people in Israel.

December 2011–January 2012 (Spokane, Washington)

Despite all the pain in our home, as the time of carols, stockings, nativities, and wrapped packages drew near, my children were elated about celebrating another holiday with all the grandparents, and we all worked hard to make sure that Jake and Lizzy had a special Christmas. Anita upgraded our Christmas tree to a full-size, and my mom decorated the hearth with garlands. Yet as our living room became a beautiful stage, covered in pines and lights, my heart was preparing for what was coming. For at this point James could barely talk, and he slept most the time in his wheelchair with his Chief Joseph wool blanket wrapped around him. As we approached the holidays, the doctor stopped his radiation but continued the chemotherapy with pills. All I really wanted for Christmas was to have our normal, everyday family life back again, but as desperately as I longed for this, it was becoming clear that we could never go back to how it had been before the cancer.

In the midst of the preparations, I convinced my in-laws, parents, and children to plan an outing so that James and I could spend some time alone together. I assured them that I would call if I needed help and excitedly planned to make our date night special.

When the night arrived, I rolled James into our narrow kitchen in his high-tech wheel chair that kept his head propped up so we could be together while I cooked. As I talked to him and asked questions, he didn't respond, and I eventually became aggravated. I missed the way he would talk to me for hours and how he would tell stories in a crowd while I sat quietly beside him. But with everything I shared with him that night, he had absolutely no response, and eventually my anger boiled with frustration and loss, and I yelled at him—something I hadn't done in a long time. His eyes popped out, which let me know that he was listening, but couldn't speak. I apologized as my heart pounded, desperately wanting him to talk to me or even yell at me. I wanted all this to be over. Later, as I spoon-fed him, we sat in silence like an old married couple. Then I administered his many medications, encouraging him to swallow each pill, but he hid them under his tongue. For more than an hour, I pleaded for him to swallow, then put him to bed. That was our last date.

Rather than singing Christmas carols or hymns each night, Lizzy started singing a song that she was writing in her heart about a desperate homeless girl whom no one would take in. The depth and despair seemed far beyond her seven years. I wondered if Lizzy was anticipating losing her dad—maybe even seeing herself as that little homeless girl. We could all see the cancer progressing, impacting James's whole being.

When Christmas finally arrived, Jake and Lizzy were full of cheer as they hopped out of bed to open presents. As their joy and chatter filled the room, I looked over and saw James in the corner, asleep in his wheelchair, totally oblivious to what was happening. I knew it was the illness, for if he'd been well, he would've been just as goofy as the kids, putting a pair of underwear on his head as he had in the past to make everyone laugh. Though he loved Christmas as much as the children, he was sleeping through this one.

I snuck away into my bedroom and sobbed, then wiped away my tears and returned to the living room to try to hold it all together.

We finally managed to get James to wake up to watch Jake play a Wii game he had received. Though they didn't interact much, I tried to take in each moment, knowing that it would probably be our last Christmas together as a family.

On top of all the emotions from the day, I had a huge decision looming ahead of me about further treatment. At his next appointment, the doctor glazed over the prognosis without giving much detail. He said they'd continue the same treatment. James Earl and Anita were sitting together as I sat next to James in his wheel chair, satisfied with what he said. All the while, I was thinking of the terrible side-effects of these drugs and wondering why James had to suffer just to extend his days to lay dormant as life passed by. Anita sensed I needed time alone with the doctor and offered that the two of them would excuse themselves.

When they left the room, I looked the doctor eye-to-eye, and I asked for the truth. "What are his chances to live?"

He looked at me for a moment and then said, "With further treatment, he has about a ten percent chance of survival."

I wondered how we could keep going through the torment of these treatments for a mere ten percent. I asked, "Then what are we doing?"

He then explained I should think about Hospice care, but if I decided to invite them in, all medical interventions to fight the cancer would have to cease.

At the time, I felt that this decision would mean giving up and letting James die. Though I wasn't ready for him to die, James had told me when we first learned about the cancer that he wanted to live fully until the end. Looking at him sleeping in the corner of the living room that Christmas, I knew that his quality of life had hit rock bottom. Though he was with us, he wasn't *there*. Though I knew that I didn't have any authority over the timing of his death, I felt like the weight of this decision was on my shoulders, since James had dictated his will to me.

Though I was afraid to say these words out loud, I knew that we couldn't keep fighting this battle. I just couldn't let James continue to be afflicted with such excruciating pain just so he could sleep through more days of life. I knew this life was not what he wanted and sensed that he was holding on for us. I tried to place my feet in his shoes and ask, *What would James do? What if I were him?* Finally, I said, "I think we need to go with Hospice."

Then James suddenly spoke up and said, "It sounds like we're quitting." His words shook me, but I knew that I had to find the courage to do what was right for James, for all of us. James had never been a quitter, but I knew that the cancer was taking over his mind. He wasn't even taking the chemotherapy pills meant to stop the cancer. I didn't want to keep holding onto his life when his death seemed inevitable. I wanted to love and support him as he left this world to be present with our Lord.

When I went to the waiting room, I shared this decision with my in-laws, who went into complete shock, as they had thought we would continue the treatments. They were very upset with me, understandably. On the way home, I stopped in our church parking lot to clear the air before we got home. They had been down this road with James as a little boy, going from doctor to doctor, believing that James would overcome the leukemia. But after four months, I was already saying, *it's time to stop and let him go.* At the time, they may have felt like I was an enemy. I had brought him out West, far away from his family, and here I was making this decision without their consultation. But as his wife and the administrator of his will, I felt the responsibility to make a decision that honored the wishes he had expressed before the cancer had eaten away so much of his brain.

As I explained all this to them, James sat quietly beside me. After this grueling conversation, we went home, completely exhausted.

Once we were inside the house, I sat next to James on our brown leather sofa— the first nice sofa we'd had, which fit well in our little old house on the South Hill. I sighed and rested my head on his shoulder, and then he said, "Heather, you did a good job." After all that we had been through, his words confirmed my decision.

I did not send out a family Christmas card that year, as our lives had been turned upside down like a snow globe. I felt comforted to remember that Mary and Joseph had not sent out fancy Christmas cards to their families and friends, either. I could relate to their family crisis, because Jesus' birth was a rough path. They had been on the road when Jesus was born, with no place to stay, and so Mary had given birth to Him, placing

Jesus in a feeding trough for animals. His baby gifts were not wrapped with red and green sparkly paper and fancy bows. Most mothers today would be offended to receive a spice for burial after giving birth—though that's what some of the wise men brought to baby Jesus (Matthew 2:11). Most parents take time off work to celebrate a new birth, but Mary and Joseph had to flee to Egypt as refugees to protect Jesus from King Herod's slaughter of newborn sons. His name, Immanuel, means God is with us. He came into a world with much agony and pain, just as He was there with us in our pain. Though the first Christmas was not ideal, it was the most miraculous occasion in world history.

Therefore the Lord himself will give you a sign.
Behold, the virgin shall conceive and bear a son, and
shall call his name Immanuel.
—Isaiah 7:14
New American Standard Bible

~ 15 ~

HIS BREATH

EVERY RIVER MUST come to an end, whether it feeds into a lake, a sea, the ocean, or splits into different tributaries. As James and I prepared to travel on different boats down streams that separated from one another, I clung to the hope of our Maker, the giver of every breath, as I let go of James.

January 2012 (Spokane, Washington)

John Henry, one of James' friends growing up in Marks, Mississippi, called about a month before Christmas to find out about James and how he could help. I encouraged him to visit and later found out that he would be coming with two other friends, Chad and Matthew. I felt so uplifted, just as I had with my sister's visit.

They arrived the first week of January, bringing so much life and a breath of fresh air into all our sorrow. They wheeled James around and sat at the dining table, telling funny stories about James late into the night. We all laughed as they told us about James's mischief—like the time he wanted stylish jeans, and so he put them over the fence and shot holes in them. Then he discovered that the air-conditioning unit was on the other side—just one of many bloopers for James. Though James was still with us, he didn't have the energy to tell stories like he had before, and so hearing them talk was like having the old James with us again. Surrounded by his old crew, he seemed to engage us all more.

Then we all decided to take a field trip to Cabela's in Post Falls, a massive retail store filled with outdoor recreation equipment. Chad, Matthew, and John Henry sat in camping chairs with Jake and Lizzy and put a wooden gun in James's lap for a snapshot. As they played with all the toys and gadgets, acting like kids, Jake and Lizzy got a glimpse of their dad again. We all belly-laughed at their goofy antics. Then we ate buffalo burgers at the cafe in the store, and Jake and Lizzy left with a few new toys from their "uncles for the day," which they played with together as soon as we got home.

We were all sad when they had to depart, and they all cried as they said goodbye to James. Matthew got down on his knees as he hugged James in his wheelchair, speaking his final words with so much grief that he finally had to go outside.

Anita was also being pressured to return to work, as she had run out of her Family Medical Leave of Absence. James Earl returned with her, which was another difficult departure. Thankfully, my parents were able to continue staying in their RV to help our family.

James was now under the care of Hospice, and I anticipated the day that I would have to say goodbye. I wrestled with how to prepare Jake and Lizzy for their father's death.

I took Lizzy on a meandering walk through our neighborhood and alongside Manito Park, gradually working up the courage to say, "Lizzy, I think your daddy is dying."

She looked up at me with her big brown eyes and curly long eye lashes and said, "Mommy, you have to believe! You have to believe Daddy can be healed."

Her words pierced my soul. I wanted to believe that God would heal James, but I knew in my heart that the healing she was looking for was probably not coming. As I thought about her words, I worried that I was not approaching his death with childlike faith. *What was God's will?* As we returned to the house, I felt awful.

Each day, every hour or so, I rolled James over to prevent bedsores. On January 28th, the day after Lizzy celebrated her seventh birthday, Lizzy and I were in the bedroom, cuddled together on the bed watching *High School Musical III*. Throughout the movie, I kept glancing at James as he slept on the hospital bed in our room like a bear in hibernation. I listened to the sound of the morphine pump and his heavy breathing, a comforting sound that told me he was still alive.

While watching the Disney story about a girl and boy falling in love, with full aspirations about their future after high school, I reflected on my own experience of falling in love. My experience had begun right out of high school—with my drive to graduate from university, marry James, and live a full life together. As I held my daughter, I saw the future of growing old with James being erased and wondered how Lizzy would be without a dad to protect her, especially during her critical teenage years. I felt like I was watching the pages of the calendar of my life with James being torn out in huge handfuls. When Lizzy fell asleep, I carried her to her room and tucked her into bed. *Would he make it one more night? Would she get to see him again the next morning?*

The next morning, Lizzy came to my room, eager to watch the movie again, though she had watched it so many times before. I didn't want to watch it, as I wanted to spend more time with James, but I gave in. As we watched the movie again, I was reminded of love, life, and dreams—all that could have been but would never be now.

After the movie and my morning cup of coffee, my mom gently reminded me that the pauses between James's breathing were stretching longer than before. I scrambled to make the atmosphere perfect for his death, as odd as that might sound. Just as I had anticipated the birth of Jake and Lizzy, I knew this moment was coming and wanted it to be special. I ran to the stereo and turned on a local Christian radio station, but they were doing an interview, so I rushed to the computer and searched for the perfect songs. I played *Finally Home* by MercyMe, a song about a son wrapping his arms around his dad's neck, telling him about the man he became and hoping it pleases him. It's about making it "home," and it parallels seeing our Father in heaven.

Knowing James was about to meet Jesus and hear the choir of angels, I played another song by MercyMe, *I Can Only Imagine*, which echoed my prayers and the indescribable encounter he was about to have, which could not be compared with climbing any summit or rafting any river. As I held onto James's frail hand, I cried over his shoulder with tears of joy, anticipating his welcome home in heaven. Would he dance? Would he fall to his knees? Would he be embraced by his brother Brandon?

As the song ended, James's lungs rose and fell, and he started to gasp for air like a fish out of water. The Hospice nurses had told me that this labored breathing was a sign that his death might be minutes away.

I asked my mom to bring in Lizzy and Jake, and when she ushered them to the bedroom door, I looked at them with a heavy heart and said, "I think Daddy is going to die today." They both stared at me, and as their tears fell, I felt like I was seeing glass shattering on concrete, with millions of fragments that would never be put together again.

"Jake and Lizzy, give Dad a hug," I told them. Our two "miracle" kids each came around his hospital bed and hugged him goodbye. As they left, I heard Jake say, "I'm playing Wii," and Lizzy said she wanted to play Sorry, a game she had enjoyed playing with her grandparents. Like my running, I realized they needed to escape the reality of this death, too.

I placed my head on his heart and listened for the heartbeat. I waited for seconds, then minutes, but it never returned.

Yahweh. This name was unspeakable by the Jews but was breathed with every inhalation and exhalation: *Yah-weh.* I breathed in and breathed out, but his breath had ceased. I could understand the cry of Job: "the Lord gave and the Lord has taken away. Blessed be the name of the Lord" (Job 1:21).

I breathed in and breathed out, but his breath had ceased.

After silent waiting, listening to the sound of my own breathing, I called Hospice to have them proclaim his death.

Looking upon James, I felt peace that he was no longer suffering. I thought, *his body is hallow. It's just a shell.* I thought about all the time we spend working to care for our bodies—buying food and clothes, heat to stay warm, soap and hair products to stay clean and fresh, dentists and doctors to maintain our decaying bodies, which are just destined for the dirt. Then I thought about the importance of investing in what lasts forever.

When Nurse Naomi arrived, I thought about how her name suited the day I became a widow. She kindly did her duties as I went to the kitchen to hide and cry. Through the blurriness of my tears, I saw James kneeling down on one knee with his thumb up, with a full smile—not the half-smile he'd had during most of his sickness because of all his seizures and the paralysis caused by the cancer. Pure, white light was shining all around him, just like the vision the girl described when she had come to pray for our family months before. The vision was like peeking through the veil of this world into heaven, and it exhilarated me.

Then I walked back to the bedroom and heard him say, "Heather, you did a good job." I welled up, because I hadn't heard his voice in weeks! Those were the words I needed to hear. Throughout our marriage, he had told me that I was the last person he'd ever want to care for him if he were sick because I was the least empathetic person he knew. He was right, but I had done a good job. I had fought the fight and run the race. Hearing those words of affirmation brought me so much peace.

Naomi called me to the dining room, because it was time for her to take the medications. I sighed as I looked in the cabinet at the rows and rows of medications that I had administered for months. Towards the end, he wouldn't swallow them, which had frustrated and exhausted me. I had wanted to give up so many times, but I had continued. Eventually, the pills had turned to liquids, then to suppositories, and then to liquid injections.

When I laid out all the bottles of medication on the table, I was relieved, but also crushed. He would no longer need these medications and would no longer suffer their many side effects. One by one, Naomi took account of our inventory, but even though I believed in his "ultimate healing," as he called it, I grieved that he no longer needed me to care for him. My job of being his wife was finished.

Then my dad arrived and quickly observed that the stress had left James's face. I was so glad to hear my dad say these words.

Jake was excited to see Poppy and wanted to be with him, and so my dad took Jake to McDonalds, his favorite restaurant, where James had often taken him and Lizzy after school for hamburgers or pancakes.

After they departed, a van pulled into our driveway, and two gentlemen knocked on our door. We welcomed them in and then stood next to the dining table as we answered their questions. They asked if I wanted to be in the room while they bagged his body, and I said, "No thanks," finding it odd to keep looking at a body that no longer housed my husband. I knew where he was now, and it was glorious!

After their work was accomplished, they rolled a maroon bag that held his body into the living room amidst Lizzy's leftover birthday decorations. Jake and Poppy returned just as they were rolling him out, and Jake started yelling, "Daddy's dead! Daddy's dead! Daddy's dead!" It was so abrupt that I didn't know what to think, but then I realized that Jake was right. His daddy was dead. He was now in heaven—and we had to come to grips that he was no longer with us on earth.

I trusted that the presence of the Lord was with us, comforting and strengthening us, though we were all in complete shock. We were watching every moment like we were living in a dramatic movie, standing in someone else's tragedy. But it was real. James was gone.

They took away his body in a van and then flew him to Mississippi to be buried next to the body of his brother, Brandon.

We all ate McDonald's lunch around the dining table, laughing as we shared precious memories from our past. My family had always handled hard times by looking for bright spots. While we reminisced, the kids barraged me with questions, even wondering if I would remarry. Though it had only been a few hours, we were all trying to put the pieces back together again. Then Lizzy asked if her daddy would get a new birthday, since he'd entered heaven that day. I savored the question and said, "Well, I guess he does, baby girl."

"Then the Lord God formed the man of dust from the ground and breathed into his nostrils the breath of life, and the man became a living creature."
–Genesis 2:7
New American Standard Bible

Then Jesus, calling out with a loud voice, said, 'Father, into your hands I commit my spirit!' And having said this he breathed his last."
–Luke 23:46
New American Standard Bible

~ 16 ~

HIS GRIEF

JUST AS RIVERS are fed by water that comes from the rains above, I have often wondered if God cries, if His tears parallel our own. Jesus certainly cried after Lazarus died, for it says in John's account of this story that "Jesus wept" (John 11:35), even though he knew that he would raise Lazarus to life. On the day James died, as rain fell from the sky, I wondered if God was shedding tears with me, giving me an image of Himself weeping with those who weep, mourning with those who mourn. Isaiah saw a vision of God's Beloved Son some eight hundred years before He walked on earth, displaying the heavy grief and sorrow He would bear: "He was despised and rejected by men; a man of sorrows, and acquainted with grief; and as one from whom men hide their faces he was despised, and we esteemed him not. Surely he has borne our griefs and carried our sorrows; yet we esteemed him stricken, smitten by God, and afflicted. But he was wounded for our transgressions; he was crushed for our iniquities; upon him was the chastisement that brought us peace, and with his stripes we are healed" (Isaiah 53:3–5).

February 2012 (Spokane, Washington)

"I know how you feel. The same thing happened to my fish," one of Jake's classmates wrote on a card, with a simple drawing of a fish floating in the water of his fishbowl. Even in our grief, this card made our family chuckle. Jake received a whole stack of cards from his classmates, which encouraged him so much that he wanted to return to school only two days after James died.

A few weeks after James's death, we sent out a simple invitation for Jake and Lizzy's classmates to attend their daddy's celebration of life. Rather than promising birthday cake and party favors, we were asking these little ones to come to mourn with my kids, but we wanted to make it a kid-friendly celebration. My friend Dawn, who had also lost her husband and been left with two children, gave me tips via email from New Zealand to help me plan the celebration.

My desire was to give every person in that room a chance to hear good news. It's easy to pass by God when giving birth or taking the tassel to the other side of a cap on graduation day, but when looking at death straight in the eye, every man and woman is confronted with their own destiny. *What is the mark, the dash, between birth and death? And what comes after?*

On the day of the celebration, all of my dear friends gathered in our home—Teri and Terese from Sandpoint, my mom and dad, so many people filled our living room to encourage us. Life filled our home!

Then we drove to Southside Christian Church to celebrate James's journey on earth and through heaven's gates. I was surprised when Jake and Lizzy didn't want to sit with me, but with their friends. I realized that I had not really been there for them, as I had been too consumed with taking care of James and my own grief, but their friends had been there.

I wept as I listened to our worship leader play acoustic guitar and sing *I Can Only Imagine* and other songs that were especially meaningful to James and me. I had made a slideshow of pictures, and it was wonderful to share our lives with those who loved us. Picture after picture revealed the full life James had lived—climbing ice, navigating rivers, being silly with his kids. One of Jake's favorite teachers, Mr. J., shared the good news in a way that spoke to Jake and Lizzy, along with all their peers. Then Pastor Rob, who had come to our home every week to share the Word with us and pray for us, stepped on stage and shared the beautiful gospel message, painted with the new life James had in Christ.

After the service, it seemed like a typical Sunday after the church service. Kids were running around the foyer, laughing and playing, as I greeted and thanked people for coming. One woman with curly blonde hair introduced herself as the mom of one of Jake's friends and shared how our story had touched her, and she had decided not to take a job that would keep her traveling extensively. She felt that being present for her family was what mattered the most. I had heard other stories about how God was touching hearts—wives who were appreciating their husbands and spending more time with them, enjoying little, everyday moments.

Another man approached me and said he'd been praying for a long time for his neighbor to come to church, but he would never come. But his son was a classmate of Jake's, and his son had brought him to church and insisted that he had to be there for his friend. So this neighbor had come and heard the gospel. I wondered if James' celebration of life had sowed a seed for one more soul to be saved in Christ.

Through it all, I clung fiercely to Romans 8:28, which says that God causes *all things* to work for the good of those who love Him and are called according to His purpose.

Many people from First Christian Church in Sandpoint also came— Pastor Kyle and his grandmother, Jake's old Sunday school teacher, and several couples from our small group. My family in Christ was paramount during this critical time.

As the church began to empty, my women's small group from Southside Christian Church stood around me in a circle, and I shared my gratitude for their presence. No one had to say a word because their presence spoke to us, and the warmth of their bodies reminded us that we were not cold, drowning, or alone. The "church" truly is the "body of Christ." All those hands, arms, and hearts helped us feel the loving embrace of Jesus.

February 2012 (Yazoo City, Mississippi)

Because both of our families were from the Southeast, we had another celebration of life for James in Yazoo City, Mississippi. The kids and I flew to Mississippi just after the service in Spokane.

As I walked into the church, I was shocked to see my cousin Brian, as I hadn't known he would come all the way from New York to be present with us, along with his younger brother, Carter, who had come from Washington D.C. Their presence touched my heart. As Brian escorted me into the church, my palms sweat, and I anxiously prepared for this service for James that was held in a place that was not my home.

The church was filled with a sea of faces that I did not recognize, apart from family members. James had grown up in the small rural town of

Marks, so there were old elementary and high school teachers, old friends and neighbors, and all the friends who had surrounded James Earl and Anita through this storm. I had to stand at the front of the church beside James Earl and Anita to greet people, and so I asked my sister to stand by my side, as I was overwhelmed by all the people I didn't know. As I shook people's hands and smiled, it almost felt like my wedding day, but rather than standing beside me, my husband was in the wooden casket covered with flowers behind me. I felt like I was the main character in a movie that I couldn't pause or rewind. I did not like all the attention, but I desired to tell James's story in order to point to the greater story about Christ.

Having flown in from the Pacific Northwest, with its shedding of traditional customs, I felt the pressure of my Southern roots pressing upon me in everyone's black clothes, the casket, all the flowers. I did not want to stare death in the face. I didn't want my children to see their daddy being lowered into the ground in a field full of old, worn stones. I quietly prayed that God would keep us from going to the burial.

After the greeting line came to an end, the pastor pulled my in-laws, sister, and me aside. He explained that there was a heavy rain that would inhibit us from going to the gravesite to bury James. I looked at my sister with eyes wide, wanting to scream, "Hallelujah!" but I only whispered, "Praise God." I felt elated that God was responding to my prayer and wanted to jump up and down, but I stilled myself, as I knew that would not be an appropriate response for a grieving widow.

During the service, I sat by Grandmother Wimberly, Anita's mom. She had short gray hair, curled like my own grandmother's, and as she rested her frail elbows on her wheelchair, I marveled at the contrast between our ages—yet we would now check the same box of "widow." As our eyes met, I felt a deep connection with her, and I knew that she understood exactly what I was experiencing and the heartache that was yet to come without saying a word.

James's cousin, Al, who was a youth pastor at the time, spoke at the service, and his sister Alletta sang. Then the senior pastor came to the stage. Having heard my kids loved the game Sorry, he eloquently used it as an analogy to explain the bigger picture of the gospel message. Then they played the slideshow of James's life. Since James had been far from Mississippi for the last twenty years, many of the people who had gathered to honor his life had never seen him with his family, living life to the fullest. They only remembered the years that they had held his hand, prayed, and walked in love beside him and his family as he fought to live.

After the service, I sat among my mom's side of the family with my sister, uncles, aunts, and cousins. As always, they looked for humor to mask the pain, but even though I found myself laughing, I felt deep sadness welling up within me, the onslaught of what would become an avalanche of despair.

I never once went to James's grave. Though it may have brought some needed closure, I had memories sprinkled across the United States and Canada, and so before returning to Washington, I decided to stop in Colorado, where our family of four had begun.

February 2012 (Copper Mt., Colorado)

I contacted my old friend, Monica, and she found us a free place to stay in the condominium that her husband, Mike, managed at Copper Mountain. As we flew into Denver after our time in Mississippi, it felt like we were going home. She and Mike picked us up at the airport and drove us along that familiar road, winding through the mountains to Frisco and then on to Copper Mountain, a two-hour drive. Monica hadn't seen Jake and Lizzy since they were babies, so it was a treat for her to see them.

Monica was the one who had consoled me over many phone conversations when her mother was dying. She had experienced the raw pain in her own life of losing her father, who had died at the age of forty-five from melanoma. Like Lizzy, she was only eight years old when he passed. She had a big heart and gladly opened her arms to receive us. Her mom had died the day after Christmas, a month before James, and she told me that the service had been standing room only, with six police cruisers and motorcycles escorting the hearse because of all the people. She described that day as the worst day of her life, and we related to one another's pain in a unique way. Our time together was a special gift for all of us.

Mike and Monica treated us like royalty, making our time there a mini-vacation before we had to step back into reality in Spokane. Despite being in such a beautiful paradise of snow, where I had begun my marriage and family with James, none of us could escape the massive hole in our lives. Our first night started out with a screeching, *"Mommy! Mommy!"*

I ran into the living room and found Jake spewing vomit everywhere. I spent the night helping him recover and cleaning up the mess on the carpet. The next day, we trudged through the snow to the medical center, and by the time he was on oxygen, his altitude sickness had dissipated. Those first two days, he despised the mountains that I loved so much and didn't ever want to return. It broke my heart to see him having such a rough start to what I had hoped would be a special time together, just the three of us, figuring out our life together without James. I had also hoped it would be a sweet time, where they could get to know their dad in a special way by being in the mountains he loved so much and meeting people who could share stories about him.

That happened when we shared a meal and caught up with Dan, who had sold our condo, and had attended our church in Summit County with his wife, Patti. They had also been on the Search & Rescue Team with James. After dinner, Dan surprised us by taking us to the Search & Rescue barn, where he gave us a grand tour and showed us old newspaper clippings of various rescues. Jake and Lizzy got to jump into one of the bright red rescue vehicles. Like James, Dan was excited to show them all the gear that they used to rescue people. As we walked down the stairs, he pointed out a picture of James and told the kids about some of the rescues he had done with him.

Another day, I took the kids dog sledding. They couldn't stop talking about how the dogs could go to the bathroom as they ran, which was the highlight for them. They also spent hours going up the hill at Copper Mountain and back down on an inner tube. They could have entertained themselves all day had it not been for bone-chilling winds and icy cold snow. To warm up, we went the Silverthorne Recreation Center, where Monica worked, and where Jake, Lizzy, James, and I used to come to enjoy indoor swimming and water slides.

What surprised me most about the whole trip was the number of people who I knew but whose stories I had never heard before, such as Monica having been raised by a single mom after her dad died from cancer. David, the husband of another old friend from the Marriott in Breckenridge, shared how he had lost his dad at a young age, and he gave me some advice about what items to hold onto for Jake and Lizzy. David had become a pro-snowboarder, and I realized that, like James who had suffered so much from his childhood cancer, David had come to the Rocky Mountains to really *live*. Rather than trying to climb the career ladder, he was seeking to live every day. He didn't take his life for granted.

Though we were only in Colorado for a few days, those days were packed full of memories and faces that I will not forget. As we left for Spokane to begin our new normal, I sadly said farewell to Mike and Monica.

As we waited in the Denver International Airport, I ran into Jody, another old friend from the Marriott. I was so moved when I saw her that I shed tears. We sat down at an airport café, and she told me about how her mother had died when she was young. With tears in her eyes, she expressed the heartaches and challenges she had experienced as a child.

While I was dealing with my own grief, I also carried the weight of how to help my children navigate this loss in their lives. I had met three people in Colorado who had experienced loss as children, and their stories gave me hope that Jake and Lizzy would be able to find their way through the loss of their father, too.

As I hugged Jody goodbye and went to catch our flight, I felt a deeper and stronger bond with all the friends we had encountered in Colorado. I knew that we were not alone on this journey of loss. God had appointed person after person to speak love and compassion into our heavy hearts.

Spring 2012 (Spokane, Washington)

After taking three weeks off work to travel to Mississippi and Colorado, I felt that I needed to return to my job. My boss encouraged me to take more time off, but I felt like they had already done too much for me by giving me time off with pay to take care of James during his sickness. I felt it was time to move on.

When we returned to Spokane, I was struck by how beautiful the house was, thanks to my parents, who had stayed to care for it. When I entered my bedroom, I realized there was no longer a hospital bed, but only the wooden bed that I had grown up with that was made by my grandfather, Bill. A picture of James caught my attention, and I picked it up and wept bitterly as I sat on my well-made bed, with every corner tucked in so nicely. But I knew my life was not that clean and tidy. In my pain, I did not want to return to this house with empty spaces, this place where my husband's body had been rolled away, and yet at the same time, I didn't want to leave. Every corner, every chair, every room was filled with memories.

The memories rolled over me like massive waves. The day I returned to work, I took my kids to school. As soon as they stepped out of the car, the levy inside me broke, and I cried all the way to work. Even the car was a reminder of James. I remembered the day we had bought it and all the days I had tried to protect his head while getting him in the front seat during his illness. Several times he had bumped his head. Everything reminded me of James.

Walking across the Spokane River after parking the car, tears continued to fall, and I felt like I had enough tears inside me to fill that river so that it would never run dry.

. . . I felt like I had enough tears inside me to fill that river so that it would never run dry.

As I reached my workplace, I stared for a moment at the big glass doors with the metal handles, wondering how I was going to do this. *How am I going to keep living when my husband is in the ground?* As I pulled open the door, I walked slowly, breathing deeply, and headed towards my cubicle. One by one, my coworkers emerged from their workstations to hug me, and as I looked at them, I was filled with gratitude. I thanked them for giving me the most precious gift of time to be with James so that I could say goodbye. My tears flowed, but the love they poured out on me that day, and over the previous months, which would continue to flow out of them in the months to come, was stronger and deeper than all my sorrow.

Sandra came downstairs day after day to ask, "How are you doing?" Her question wasn't a casual greeting, but a deep-rooted question about my soul. Her soft voice always reminded me that God never stopped caring for me. She continued to wake up early to run with me each week and to listen to my heartache.

Another coworker, Alisha, had accompanied me through James' sickness, giving me advice about where to go for the best care and what to expect, as she had journeyed through brain cancer with a close relative. Whenever she came downstairs and placed her hand on my shoulder, I knew she was behind me, for in her touch I felt an overwhelming sense of love.

These seemingly insignificant moments of life were powerful reminders of God's love. Each touch, hug, and listening ear was a sign of God's care for me. I felt that He saw every tear of mine drop to the ground—ground that was also mourning and groaning for His return to make everything right again.

Day after day, I worked on my computer, responding to emails, and preparing for one meeting after another. Work was a false escape from the massive tomb that stuck to me like a tattoo. My job required lots of networking, so I constantly met with people who were compassionate, but again and again, I had to confront the word "death." The subject of my family, which had been so natural in casual conversation, was now a bitter herb that stuck in my teeth. In any conversation, after sharing that I had two children, I would stumble over my words, saying "we," or "our," and then I would realize, *he's not here. I'm no longer an us. I'm a me.* Or there would be an innocent question, such as, "What does your husband do?" and I'd reply with a bomb of an answer: "He died." This would be followed by an embarrassed and awkward, "I'm sorry," and then the person would quickly figure out an exit strategy. It was a quick conversation killer.

I had always felt creative and inspired at work, but now I felt hollow. I was haunted by the vanity of it all—the way businesses kept trying to sell more and more products, how so many employees gave so much of their time and energy to keep these businesses growing and thriving while they bypassed their families. The daily dramas that the women around me talked about seemed so trivial, and as I contemplated my own role and purpose in life, I felt that everything seemed like chasing after the wind, as the writer of Ecclesiastes so eloquently describes. Every day, I asked myself, *why am I here?* And everyday, I got in my car after a long day of work and cried all the way home. My children kept asking, "Mommy, why are you crying?" And I would reply, "You know why."

I decided to work out more than my mere five miles of running each week, so I got a pass to the YMCA, which gave me a perfect little vacation from the climactic drama that never seemed to end. Like a hamster on a wheel, I pounded on the treadmill, feeling the raw intensity of my grief, with no end in sight—no aim, no destiny. While I sweated bullets, I read books about tragic loss, which reminded me that I was not alone. Though I was surrounded by people in the gym, every story I read hit me at the core, and I sobbed and sobbed as I continued to run, wiping the salty tears off my face.

Every Friday night, Jake, Lizzy, and I watched movies with popcorn—a weekly family favorite tradition. It seemed every movie we watched was about someone dying or some other great loss, giving us all an occasion to cry in the darkness. We watched *Soul Surfer* and *Courageous* over and over again, reminding ourselves to keep going and keep living.

When I received an invitation to a Hospice Celebration of Roses at the Spokane Lincoln Center, I felt I had experienced enough funerals for the year, but after being encouraged to attend in my grief counseling, I decided the celebration would be good for our family. I had attended Chamber functions at the Lincoln Center before, but now I would be there to mourn.

Upon entering there was a table covered in roses, where I placed a picture of James among other photos of loved ones who had died. Many were old and faded, but ours was a fresh and recent picture of a young man. It just didn't seem right.

We found a place to sit, and as we waited, I became anxious about how Jake and Lizzy would respond. Then an elderly woman sat beside us, kindly greeted us, and as we began conversing with low voices in the quiet room, we learned that her husband had died and had spent more than thirty years as a public school bus driver. My children immediately became interested and began talking about Hutton Elementary School, as it meant so much to them.

A choir of young women dressed in red found their positions on the bleachers on stage and then began to sing a beautiful melody filled with word pictures of death as a sailboat heading towards the sunset. While I sat there weeping, I looked at Lizzy, who was on my right, ferociously coloring a Care Bear in blue crayon, not even trying to stay in the lines, which was unusual for her. On my left, Jake, who had been told by his daddy over and over again to be tough and not cry, was completely broken, letting it all go. His sorrow overflowed like burst water pipes. He had not only lost his dad, but his best friend. A few girls in the choir looked down at him as they sang, and I could tell that they were on the verge of tears. I wondered how they managed to sing for all these grieving people.

Looking at my kids, I understood that my grief would be strongest now, but theirs might be the strongest in years to come—the day when his absence would be most felt. Who would walk Lizzy down the aisle on her wedding day? Who would give Jake those talks through puberty and all those stages of becoming a man? What about father-daughter dances, Jake's first touchdown, graduation, and fatherly advice when they had their own children?

Each of us continued to attend individual counseling. Jake typically buried people in the sand during play therapy. I talked through the thousands of thoughts that churned through my head each day as I tried to function in society. Lizzy avoided counseling completely, but I later learned that her greatest counselors were her friends on the playground. One day she told me she and her friends had a funeral during recess. I asked who it was for, and she said a flower had died. Certainly our friends and people who cared about us were the greatest comforters through this trauma.

Every night, Jake, Lizzy, and I cuddled in bed together. They held me tightly, holding onto the only parent they had left. Sensitive to my fragile state, they were always at peace with one another and did their best to make sure I was okay. I didn't drop out as a parent, but I knew that we were living in a glass house, where it seemed that one wrong move might shatter an entire room. I also knew that even if I tried to keep the doors of that glass house closed, Jake and Lizzy could see everything.

As Jesus was fully human, "a man of sorrows" who was "acquainted with grief" (Isaiah 53:3), I knew that we were not alone in our sadness. I trusted that I could express all of my messy, raw emotions before Him and those He placed around us, many of whom had also traveled this valley, too. These friends walked with us, held our hands, mourned alongside us, and were Christ to us.

Blessed be the God and Father of our Lord Jesus Christ, the Father of mercies and God of all comfort; who comforts us in all our affliction so that we may be able to comfort those who are in any affliction with the comfort with which we ourselves are comforted by God.
—2 Corinthians 1:3–4
New American Standard Bible

～ 17 ～

HIS INHERITANCE

THERE IS A lot of equipment when it comes to river guiding—the boat, paddles, ropes, throw bags, food containers, dry bags, life jackets, and quick-dry clothes for frigid waters. James's inheritance to us was a garage filled with all types of gear, but what we valued was not his stuff, but the life he lived, the lessons he taught, and the faith he so boldly proclaimed, especially in those months before he passed.

March 2012–October 2012 (Spokane, Washington)

I peered through the window as a man approached our house. With his head hanging low and covered by a ball cap, I couldn't make out who he was. I twisted the doorknob and opened the door, and he handed me a large netted bag filled with baseballs, bats, and footballs. Then he walked away without a word, his head still facing the ground. When I saw the brown hair curling up under his ball cap, I woke up and realized that I had been dreaming about my brother-in-law, Brandon. I felt angry that Brandon had taken his own life. He could've been here in this critical time for Jake and Lizzy, teaching Jake techniques for the football field and introducing Lizzy to the sports he loved. He had never even gotten the chance to meet them!

I knew that I needed to forgive Brandon, just as the pastor from my childhood church had preached on television while I was lying awake in Brandon's bedroom after his funeral. But his absence from our lives was another loss I had to grieve.

I felt caught in between two worlds—one with James and one without. I still wore my wedding band on my left ring finger, and I often found myself twisting it around and around. Time seemed to stand still, but all the memories continued to circle in my mind, tainted with pain rather than joy. As I turned the wedding band, I wondered what to do with it. James had never worn his, because it was uncomfortable and irritating on his thick finger. But I had worn this ring for nearly twelve years and had rarely taken it off. It was a constant reminder of my commitment to him through the scratches and tarnish of our marriage.

I decided that I wanted to keep wearing it as a symbol of my commitment to Jesus. I wanted others to know that I was taken—He is mine, and I am His. As I pondered and cried, I realized I was afraid of letting go, saying goodbye, admitting that I was no longer married to James. I will always be committed to Jesus, but my vows with my earthly husband were "until death do we part."

One day I decided to connect with Jerry Sittser, the author of one of the books I had read called "A Grace Disguised: How the Soul Grows through Loss", who just so happened to live in Spokane. His story touched me deeply. He met me at the Service Station, and as we sat drinking coffee, one of his first observations was that I didn't wear a wedding band. He nodded, speaking kindly and thoughtfully, that I was moving forward. He had moved on, marrying again. As I contemplated this further, I knew that if God sent the right man, I too would want to remarry, just as James had encouraged me shortly after his diagnosis, but to do this, I had to let go of my first husband.

In the depths of despair, I was continuously reminded that I was still living on earth. James had gone home, but Jake, Lizzy, and I were still on earth. In their grief, Jake and Lizzy would sometimes say that they wanted to die like their daddy, or they wished it was them instead of him. Their words reflected what I felt inside, too.

I was filled with hope that James had received the ultimate healing and was now at home with Jesus (2 Corinthians 5:8). But the emptiness in our house felt enormous as Jake, Lizzy, and I sat at our banged-up dining room table night after night, staring at James's empty chair. I deeply longed to be at the King's table with James sitting by my side.

I didn't miss all the grand experiences we'd shared as much as the little, ordinary details of life. As I slept alone each night, I craved to feel his arms around me. Though he had been a tough man, he had loved to cuddle, and I'd always felt secure with him by my side. I missed his constant breathing and even his snoring during allergy season. I stared at the empty office chair in our bedroom and reminisced about sitting on his lap and the conversations we'd shared. And though it used to annoy me, I missed receiving his phone calls to make sure I was okay while walking downtown to my car. I even missed picking up his Monster drinks at the grocery store. I missed his smell, his encouragement, his love—everything. The mail still came addressed to him, and every form that I completed for the children asked for their father's name.

We had been "one flesh," and now my body felt like it had been torn apart, split in two, and my heart felt like it was made of broken shards of glass that kept scratching against one another. I wondered, *how do I become whole again?* Death had robbed me of joy and laughter, but I held on tightly to hope as I walked through the valley of grief, trusting that joy would come after mourning.

Then, a month or two after James died, I received a note on the door of our rental house, informing me that the owner had defaulted his loan. I had to make a decision either to buy the house, which had constant reminders of James, or to move on. After much prayer and counsel from friends from our church, I knew I had to let go. Rather than holding onto the past, I had to keep going forward, trusting God to guide and defend me. Though I had lost the covering of my husband, God was taking care of our family through what we still had—one another and our friends at work, church, and the children's school. And most importantly, I had Him.

I didn't have to look far to see how many blessings had poured out of the dark clouds of our grief since James had died. In time, as God continued to provide for us and breathe life into us, I trusted that light would return, and we would all begin to see the magnificent rainbow forming above us.

As I prepared to move, I had to go through all of James's belongings. In the basement, I wept over his life jacket, which still smelled of the rivers we had paddled together. Sifting through his many tubs of gear was overwhelming, but I felt certain that James would want me to sell everything to help support our family. For several weeks, I came home after work each evening and carried loads up the stairs to get ready for a big yard sale. The living room started to look like a reality TV show about people who didn't know how to throw stuff away. I couldn't believe how much we had accumulated! My friend Katherine kindly helped me sort through everything to get ready for the yard sale. She understood that I was also sorting through reminders and memories. There were some items that I couldn't bear to sell—like the shoes I put on his feet day after day to go to radiation or his favorite Patagonia fleece, which I had curled up against so many times, feeling its worn softness as his arms wrapped around me.

On the day of the sale, our yard became a retail store of all the quality gear that James had gathered across the country. As a sweet old couple purchased some items, they smiled and commented about how high-end everything was—not your typical yard sale junk. After I shared about James's death, they went through everything again and purchased more, genuinely concerned.

But one man picked up my husband's shoes and haggled over the price. I was not in any state to negotiate prices, and so I sternly put my foot down and refused. When he left, I thought, *I didn't want that man wearing my husband's shoes anyway.* It was the wrong attitude, but I knew that whatever we received, however small, would be part of our inheritance from James. I later realized why people hire others to do estate sales, as it was an extremely difficult process to go through in that first year after his death.

While bargaining all day, I reflected on all the time James had spent hunting for deals—and now it was merely a pile of cheap rubbish in our front yard. I had never liked the clutter. He seemed to have three pairs of everything just in case there was a major catastrophe! But even though he'd prepared for WWIII, he hadn't prepared for the tragedy of our own family's loss. Without James, his stuff meant nothing. I was sobered by all the waste and just wanted to get rid of all of our belongings, jump in an RV, and travel with the kids across the country. All our possessions seemed absolutely worthless, like fool's gold.

After the sale, life seemed to move forward like a slow-motion picture. But through all the raindrops that continued to fall from the sky, I began to see fragments of color. One day, while sitting at work, I got a call from the hospital where James had received his radiation treatments. I knew that I still owed nearly $6,000, but the woman told me that I did not owe anything because the hospital was taking care of the bill. I thanked her, hung up, and then burst into tears of thankfulness. Then I jumped out of my chair to tell my co-workers the news. That blessing felt like one more step towards freedom from all the bills and other concerns that were weighing us down. We continued to receive gifts from people all over the US, and through their provision, our financial burden was lifted.

A gentleman from our church also came to help us mow the lawn each week, and my friends helped out with Jake and Lizzy when I needed it. My friend Terese even took her spring break vacation as a teacher to come watch Jake and Lizzy so that I could continue to work. Again and again, I was reminded that blessings were people, not things. Though my loneliness felt like a kind of poverty, God was present to me and demonstrated his love to me through the saints who were intentionally present to me in this season.

> *I was reminded that blessings were people, not things.*

Though we had always thought of that little house on Grand Boulevard as our home, God gave us a new beginning in a duplex a few blocks away with new bedrooms, new white carpet, a new landlord, and new neighbors. The day I met the landlord, he told me that the woman who had lived there previously had died at home with the support of Hospice. While he might have thought that would deter me from living there, I felt it was a sign. I wanted our family to bring new life into that space.

Several months after we moved, I drove by our old home and saw blue light flashing from the TV on the mantle. Through the big glass windows of that old house, I could see a dining room table. A car was parked in the driveway. Life had continued there, too, and it made me wonder if the new family knew the story of our family.

It wasn't easy to let go, and it was a process that would take years and possibly a lifetime. I continued to dream of James. Sometimes he'd be divorcing me, and then I'd wake up and remember, *Oh, he's dead.* Every time I woke up from this dream, I felt baffled when I realized that he was gone.

I knew that I needed wisdom and comfort during this tumultuous time, and so I joined a GriefShare at a nearby church, where I met Tristin, a woman about my age who had recently lost her husband and been left with a son to raise. We sat side by side every week, crying, as we listened to others who had been through loss. We were reminded of what the Bible says about grief and how to deal with belongings, finances, and other practical tips. Tristin and I started to meet at the local gym to exercise while talking through our emotions.

After finishing GriefShare, Tammie, a widow at Southside Christian Church who had been reaching out to me after James's death, asked if I might help her start a GriefShare at the church. I agreed, and began meeting more people who had experienced loss and accompanying them down the rapids of grief with all its twists and turns.

During my first year as a widow, I began searching the Scriptures for passages and stories about widows. I was drawn to James 1:27: "This is pure and undefiled religion in the sight of our God and Father, to visit orphans and widows in their distress, and to keep oneself unstained by the world." I was stirred by the way that God calls Himself "a father of the fatherless and a judge for the widows" (Psalm 68:5).

As I contemplated the story of Elisha and the widow in distress in 2 Kings 4:1–2, I realized that I was like the widow at the beginning of the story, for sometimes all I noticed was the emptiness of our house. Yet when Elisha asks her, "Tell me, what do you have in the house?" she recognizes that she has one jar of oil. Elisha's question helps her focus on what she has and the God who can fill that empty space, rather than on what she lacks. Elisha tells her to borrow empty vessels, and then her one jar of oil miraculously fills as many empty vessels as she brings. Then Elisha instructs her to go sell the oil to pay her debt to the creditors and support her family with the rest. God saves her two children from slavery and protects her family from poverty by filling those jars with oil.

As I reflected on God's heart for widows and the fatherless, I began to realize that losing the head of the household during biblical times didn't only involve loss and grief, but also caused many other difficulties. In the agrarian society of the ancient first world, people didn't have social security or social services, and so the widows and fatherless were especially vulnerable to abuse, poverty, and even death. But throughout the biblical narrative, God demonstrated His tenderness towards them. I trusted that He would demonstrate tenderness to our family by protecting and supporting us, too.

I also thought about how God brought Ruth, a foreign widow, into Naomi's family through Boaz so that her dead husband's name would not be cut off from his inheritance (Ruth 4:10). Then Ruth became the great grandmother of David, who became a forefather of Jesus, who was God's great inheritance to all people.

As I encountered all the Scriptures that demonstrated God's special care for widows and orphans, along with the importance of sharing the gospel message to the nations, I began to ask, *Lord, what do I do now?* I kept remembering James's words before his death, about how he wanted us to serve God more.

Later in that first spring without James, a woman came up to me after one of Jake's programs at church and introduced herself to me. She offered her condolences and said that she had heard our story through her son, who had become friends with Jake that year. I shared about the miraculous work God had done in James's heart before he died. As we talked, I learned that her family was on a year-long furlough from Brazil, and they were preparing to return to a different mission field. My heart leaped, and I shared my longtime desire to serve in missions, which had been sparked after my first mission trip to Guatemala when I was fourteen. Rather than shy away or discourage me, she fanned the flame that had been slowly burning in my soul.

I began to pray, "Lord, send me." I desperately wanted to pass along the great inheritance that I had received, but I had no idea that what I was asking for would change my life so dramatically.

After much prayer, discussions with my pastor, and taking a class called Perspectives, I had the opportunity to attend large missions conference in Spokane. I was full of excitement from the many ways He had prepared the way for me to come. One of the keynote speakers didn't show, and in his place, a tall African man came on the stage and introduced himself as Emmanuel. He shared how he had lost thirty-five family members in the genocide against the Tutsi in 1994 in his home country of Rwanda.

His powerful testimony was one of hope and forgiveness. He shared about a ministry he had begun that reached out to widows and orphans. The ministry was founded upon James 1:27, which speaks about caring for widows and orphans in their distress.

After he spoke, I went to him in tears and explained my own heartache for widows and shared a bit of my story. He compassionately listened and empathized. I then shared my desire to be in missions and about my prayers that last year. He said their ministry team had been praying for the last year and half for a missionary to join their work.

He suggested that I speak to someone named TJ, who was at the booth for their ministry. Overwhelmed by how God had orchestrated every detail, I approached the booth, where I introduced myself to a lady with blond hair and a big smile. As I shared my passion and story, some tears started to flow, and she stopped me mid-sentence and asked, "Excuse me, what did your husband die from?"

I responded, "Glioblastoma multiforme."

"My husband died from the same cancer," she said and then explained how she wasn't supposed to be in Spokane but had suddenly come to help with this event. She explained how she ran an organization called Apple of His Eye Charity, which supports widows and orphans through their ministry and others. We ended up having lunch, and when I met again with Emmanuel, I realized that I had the business start-up, communication, and management skills he was looking for. We were all bewildered by the astonishing ways God had brought us all together that day.

Before I knew it, I was on a plane to the heart of Africa. Those empty spaces within me were being made whole as He poured into me through so many people.

I pray that the eyes of your heart may be enlightened, so that you may know what is the hope of His calling, what are the riches of the glory of His inheritance in the saints.
—Ephesians 1:18
New American Standard Bible

~ 18 ~

HIS HEALING

AT SOME POINT every river guide will deal with wounds: scrapes, bloody noses, broken bones, and sometimes even death. As I paddled into new territory in the heart of Africa, traveling and encountering various people and their stories, I began to understand more richly about Jesus as healer. As I witnessed the need for healing in the small nation of Rwanda, I also recognized my own need for it—not only after the loss of James, but for all the other untreated wounds I had accumulated through crashing waves that pounded against me. I felt as if I had been planted in a garden and was growing like a little mango tree out of the ashes as God placed me at the fringe of many graves.

January 2014 - December 2015 (Spokane, WA to Kigali, Rwanda)

Love made me do some crazy things—like plunging into the raging Ocoee River just to be with James. He had beckoned me to come out from behind the camera, away from the edges of the river. In a similar way, most of my walk with Christ had been on the sidelines. I imagined myself out there in the action, but I knew that I needed to take a risk and jump into the water, becoming sopping wet from head to toe.

One of James's final words of encouragement to me was, "When life throws you a curve ball, hit a home run." After he died, I asked myself, *do I want to dip in or go deep? Do I want a mediocre relationship with God or a radical, dynamic relationship?* Little by little, I felt God ushering me to go beyond the rapids into a new territory, with a new language, new people and a completely different context. I feared being uncomfortable, unsafe, and unequipped for this journey, but in July 2013, I left my children with family, got on a plane, and headed over the Atlantic Ocean to immerse myself in a three-week vision trip.

After transferring planes on African soil for my final destination, the woman sitting next to me asked why I was going to Rwanda. When I mentioned the ministry, she said that the man she had sat with on the previous plane was going to serve with them as well and then introduced me to Mike, who greeted me with a big smile. He told me he was coming to capture photos and video footage to help support them. *Interesting*, I thought. I love photography! I also learned he was from Seattle, which is not too far from Spokane. *Crazy*, I thought, but God is always full of wonderful surprises—even providing me with a little taste of home.

When we landed in Kigali, Mike and I stood in line together and chatted with excitement about the weeks ahead. He shared how he had adopted a boy from Ethiopia and had provided photography for other Christian organizations. As a first-timer in Africa, I soaked in all the joys he expressed from his travels to different countries on the continent.

While we talked and waited in the immigration line, adjusting to the humidity that was so unlike the Northwest, I realized I was also waiting for a revelation, a word from God. *Is this where Jake, Lizzy, and I are supposed to come join You?* While we had received many confirmations; I still desired one more.

The next morning, Mike and I ate little bananas and pancakes with honey on top and then walked to the nearest bus stop, squeezed in with the crowds, and sat hip-to-hip with others as we made our way to Christian Life Assembly Church that we'd been invited to attend. Sitting on the small bus, I would grow to love the closeness of people everywhere I went, being constantly touched, kissed, and hugged.

Looking out the window, I could see many people walking in large groups, carrying Bibles under their arms as they headed to church. The girls were all wearing what looked like prom dresses from the 1980s, and the men were wearing suits and ties. *Where am I?* I wondered. I had never seen people walking with Bibles under their arms in Spokane—nor anywhere in the States, though I felt a tinge of familiarity with my upbringing in the Bible belt.   .

We entered the huge church and enjoyed an entire service in English, which gave me hope that there would be options for my children and me to adapt to life here. Worshipping with people from many nations was like a foretaste of heaven, where all tribes will gather before the throne (Rev. 7:9).

Later in the week, we met a group of widows and their daughters who met regularly at one of their homes in Kicukiro, an area in Kigali, to make various handcrafts to support one another. They had passed through the genocide against the Tutsi together and were committed to consoling each other and walking this journey of grief together.

Upon entering the rusty red iron sheet door, the women stood up to greet us with a hug, touching us cheek-to-cheek three times, then shaking our hands. They returned to sit on a mat on the ground and continued weaving bowls with brightly colored threads made from banana leaves, and the bowls popped with color, mirroring the life I saw springing up all over this land. Birds were nesting and taking off from the iron roof above, making clanging noises as they came and went. Chickens were running around, and children burst in and out of the front door.

After hearing their story as a group, I shared my story of widowhood and could see the empathy on their faces. After our brief but deeply touching encounter, I felt comfort from these older widows, who embraced me as if I were their daughter. One even advised me to remarry, as she regretted that she had not remarried herself.

Before we were about to leave, I asked them for a new name. Though I didn't know it at the time, names have great significance in Rwanda, where they have large naming ceremonies for their babies. The women huddled together, whispering and discussing what they might name me, and then proudly came forth with *Uwamahoro*, which means someone who comes in peace. I was excited to accept this powerful new name that Rwandans could understand and pronounce, as the "th" in "Heather" is a difficult sound that doesn't exist in Kinyarwanda.

A couple of weeks later, Mike and I attended another local church where we were ushered to the front to be seated on the stage, which I really disliked, but I understood that this was how they showed hospitality to their visitors. People were wearing their "Sunday best" (as we say in the Southeast US), with the men in white-collared shirts and slacks and the women wearing the bright colors of a local fabric called *kitenge*. Everyone was dancing, singing, and moving their feet to the beat of the electric keyboard as they praised God's name. As I joined them in worship, I was saturated by the intensity of it all.

During the service, various individuals came forward to share a word or praise that they had received from God. One woman came forward, closed her eyes, and began to walk to and fro, speaking loudly and passionately as she moved around. When she started approaching me, I grew timid and then felt scared as she cradled her arms under my legs and around my shoulders as if to pick me up. *What is this woman saying and why is she rocking me like a baby?* I wondered, for she was speaking over me, but I could not understand her words. After she let go, I tried to listen and prayed, *God, what are You saying to me?* but I couldn't hear anything and felt baffled.

The next day, Emmanuel and I sat in Gisenyi on Lake Kivu near Goma, DRC, where we could hear the sounds of firing because of our proximity to the border. The sun had set, and I was anxious to hear him translate what had been spoken over me. I was growing impatient, which was something I desperately needed to work on. Then we sat face to face, and he warned me to test the spirits because there were many false prophets, but as I listened to his translation, I only heard words of love and affirmation. One of the final words she spoke is that God would bless me in my obedience to Him.

Days later when Mike and I were back in Kigali, I shared what God was stirring in my heart. I was still not quite sure if I should move our family to Kigali. Mike said, "Heather, it seems pretty clear."

With his words, I knew it was time to push beyond my doubts and come to Rwanda. God was calling my family to join Him in this beautiful nation that had been widowed and orphaned as we had been.

When I returned to Spokane and spoke to pastor Galen at Southside Christian Church, I shared my new Rwandan name, *Uwamahoro*. He responded, "You know, in Hebrew, the word *peace* is translated *shalom*, which means wholeness." He said that perhaps God was going to bring wholeness to me in Rwanda. His words sunk deep into my heart.

I continued to work full-time at the chamber while prayerfully moving forward towards the call I felt to Rwanda, writing letters to family and friends to share the vision for serving there. A couple of months later, I got a huge surprise when my cousin sent a gift of $7,000, the needed funding for the plane tickets. The day I received it was pivotal, as I was assured that God would provide for our every need, as He had during James's illness and after his death. After receiving this gift, I turned in my two-week notice to one of the best jobs and teams I had ever had.

I felt motivated to sell and give away nearly everything we had, which seemed even wilder than falling in love with James or jumping off cliffs with a rope and harness. The strappings of money, living paycheck to paycheck, and having a poverty mentality always held James and I back from starting anything new. We didn't work for the fancy house or cars, but our idols were recreational sports. In living in the most natural, wild places, we had to compete with the living expenses of the wealthiest. Most all of our income went to the basics - rent, food, health, childcare, and of course our toys to live an adventure in the outdoors. Quitting my job and getting rid of possessions was a real heart-check. *Did I really trust God?* I moved forward, confident that I was fastened and secure in the palm of God's hand and that He would care for our needs. I knew He was inviting me to join Him, which was an invitation I did not want to turn down.

Over the next weeks and months, our church and various individuals began to offer support for us in faith, through prayer, financial gifts and in other tangible ways. My friend Tammie, who had led and continued leading GriefShare at our church, invited us to live with her family until we left, which alleviated us from the burden of having to pay high rental rates. She was on the final track of attaining a degree to work as a nurse. Her family invested in us by their loving presence in our daily lives, as we shared in evening meals together and on the weekends, between the busy school schedules. Her young adult children, who had lost their dad, would hang out, watch movies, cook together or play games with Jake and Lizzy; and often Tammie and I would sit in her living room drinking cappuccino and processing life moving on without our husbands by our sides.

I also saw God's presence and work in Jake's life, as he kept persisting that he wanted to be baptized. Before leaving our church family in Spokane, he committed his life to Jesus and was baptized before the congregation. Though Jake didn't want to move to Africa, he obediently followed and yielded to the Father's will.

We left Spokane with six suitcases and flew to see my family in

Chattanooga before heading off to Rwanda. We stayed with my sister and her family, where we rested before the journey ahead. During that time, I had an opportunity to revisit the Ocoee River, where James and I had made so many memories. I took a drive by myself and sat on a rock on the bank of the river, where I watched the water flow. I sobbed over that familiar river, where James was no longer by my side. I began reading in Joshua 1: "Now it came about after the death of Moses the servant of the Lord that the Lord spoke to Joshua the son of Nun, Moses' servant, saying, 'Moses My servant is dead; now therefore arise, cross this Jordan...'" (Joshua 1:1–2a).

In that moment, I knew God was speaking to me through His living Word. I needed to arise and go! Though James was dead, I was still alive. It was time to cross the river with my children. This was another pivotal moment that helped me take the risk to plunge my feet into Kigali, Rwanda.

Only a week later, I was sleeping in a hotel room in Atlanta with my dad, Lizzy, and Jake. As I lay in the dark room, I had this incredible picture of God's magnificent hand covering us. Like little chickens under their mom's wings, we were being protected and sheltered by the Almighty God. As I drifted off to sleep that night, our last on American soil for a while, I had this overwhelming sense of God's love and care for us.

On January 29, 2014, two years after James went to be with the Lord, Jake, Lizzy and I landed in Rwanda. As our plane descended, I was struck by the way the nation looked like one big garden, so lush and green. As we embarked on this fresh new chapter before us, I felt completely surrounded by the embrace of Southside Christian Church in Spokane, Stuart Heights Baptist Church in Chattanooga, and our family and friends who had stood by us through tragedy and were now accompanying us in faith as we traveled to this foreign land.

We exited the aircraft in Kigali and began settling in, establishing relationships with people who did not know our story. We first lived with a family member of Emmanuel's, enjoying her family's presence and getting a glimpse into a different way of life. They had prepared a room for us, assembling a bunk bed so that we could stay. The home had marble floors, a front porch, a beautiful garden in front with brightly colored flowers and grass, and two kitchens, one inside and an outdoor kitchen. There was a long strip in the back of the house where cooking and cleaning laundry took place.

We quickly learned that hot showers—and sometimes cold ones—didn't always come from the faucet. When water was running low in the area, jerry cans had to be purchased. Washing clothes by hand and hanging them in the sun required time, much more than we were used to, and buying food, preparing it, and cooking over charcoal was a full-day process. Jake and Lizzy watched our host family ring the neck and chop off the head of the chicken for dinner and got to pet the goat before it was taken to be slaughtered for the feast that night. There was no need for recycling bins, as recycling was a way of life—tires became toys for kids, banana leaves turned into soccer balls, and soda was always sold in reused bottles, with the lids saved to make handcrafts. Nothing went to waste! Life generally felt more raw and real, unlike the bubble-wrapped, ready-to-eat meals we had grown accustomed to in the States.

In that first month, Emmanuel had arranged with the local government to distribute goats to the poorest families in Nyamata and would provide veterinary visits to help them breed goats. It was an official ceremony at their head office where sixty people sat on narrow wooden benches before the leaders. After the officiality of the meeting concluded, Emmanuel requested Jake close with a prayer. Jake confidently went before them and prayed that the people would be grateful for the goats, but more importantly that they would be thankful for the blood of the Lamb that was slain for them. I was amazed at the movement of the Holy Spirit within him! An old man put his hands on Jake's shoulders, smiling with glee, touched by his prayer. Afterwards we walked with everyone to the little house where the goats were kept, and Jake and Lizzy stood amidst them as they were distributed one by one.

As we continued staying with our host family, we waited for Emmauel's home to be ready, as they had current renters. One day Lizzy's young teacher, an American single lady, asked us if we wanted to live with her and her roommates until it was ready. We took her offer and lived with her and an Australian couple for more than a month in a quaint three-bedroom house. Jake slept on their couch with a mosquito net, and Lizzy and I snuggled under our net on a twin bed. The house was always full of activity, with rotating security guards, a house worker, and various friends stopping by, along with a little zoo of rabbits, a turtle, chickens, and a dog named Dingo.

An American minister, who was called Pr. "Robot" (Pr. Robert), also befriended us. He often stopped by the office as he passed through to preach in the local markets. He invited our family over for dinner to share his tales of living in Africa, treating us with delicious food cooked on the grill.

Only after a few months of being in Rwanda, I got a shocking message from my friend Peter: "My condolences to you about your friend." The news reported he had died in his bed and was discovered by his neighbors after they noticed a stench coming from his home. There was absolutely no explanation of his death. There were suspicions, but it was a baffling mystery. I hadn't known the minister very well, but Jake, Lizzy, and I found ourselves at his gravesite with Emmanuel and a few of his friends, watching his simple wooden casket being lowered into the ground among thousands of other graves. That was the first of many experiences that took me to the edge of the grave.

We eventually were able to settle into a house and hired a security guard to sit at our gate at night and another lady Diana who would live with us, take care of the home and help us navigate life. She even planted some crops in our backyard and introduced us for the first time to the guava fruit growing in our back yard. Attending to the daily rhythms, I was drawn to the cleanliness. Diana was always cleaning me off, literally dusting off my pants when I left the house, telling me I can't leave the house with dust on my pants. Upon exiting the gate each day, I rarely ever saw trash along the road. As a whole the nation bans plastic bags, and I was warned never to throw anything out of the car window (which was a delight to hear, as I shared this same value of keeping the environment clean). Diana always brought food from the markets in large rice bags, carrying them on the back of motorcycles which was always impressive, and then she carefully cleaned it all before placing it in the refrigerator. Every month, community members came together for *Umuganda*, where they worked together to clean their area, repair roads, and attend community meetings. The city was developing fast, perhaps growing faster than any nation in Africa.

But behind this veil of beauty and order was an invisible spiritual war, just like in every place around the world. Nearly twenty years earlier, people had been fed lies and propaganda to hate and kill an entire people group, the Tutsi, with machetes and other farming tools, and this war of rape and torture sporadically popped up in everyday conversations. As we adjusted to our new surroundings, the reality of the aftermath of the genocide in the country settled like a dark cloud around us.

While Jake, Lizzy and I were eating dinner one evening, Diana explained in detail the horror of how her own father had been killed. He had had no proper burial, like so many during those one hundred days. A few years later, her mother died from health issues, leaving Diana to be raised by extended family. The whole nation had suffered similar stories of pain and agony.

During the memorial week of the genocide against the Tutsi in April, I witnessed a woman running on the sidewalk, naked except for the panties she wore. She flew by my car door in a flash. Shocked, I wondered if she had been raped and was trying to escape her abuser. But before I could react, she was gone.

When I reached home, I shared what I had witnessed with Diana. After expressing my bewilderment, she spoke softly, "Heather, do you not know what happened here?"

My heart sunk. "Yes, of course I do."

She replied, "That's what people do. They strip off their clothes and run." She explained that when some of her people remember, they often throw off their clothes and bolt, as if reliving the trauma over again.

Due to the many visitors to our ministry, I often visited memorials with them and frequently took them to one in Nyamata which was formerly a Catholic church. Ten thousand people fled to escape the genocide, but rather than offering sanctuary to the desperate people, they were handed over to be slaughtered by their attackers. The bullet holes, blood splattered on the walls, and remains of clothes are still there to remind people of what happened and to proclaim to the world, "Never again!", which was often inscribed on a white ribbon around the flowers left upon memorials throughout the country.

With every visit to Nyamata, I saw the same woman sweeping the memorial. I was told she lost her entire family, and every day she spends her time cleaning the grounds. The passage from Ecclesiastes: "It is better to go to a house of mourning than to go to a house of feasting, because that is the end of every man, and the living takes it to heart" (7:2).

The loss of one million lives is too hard to fathom, because even the loss of one is too much to bear. As I watched Rwandans tend their memorials and grave sites during the month of April each year, I entered their heartache and sorrow. Rwandans taught me the importance of remembering, as they gathered in every village every April to share testimonies from the war so that the history would be passed down, never to be repeated. Even today there are still those who deny that it happened, despite the astonishing evidence and many survivors. As they mourned their family members, I also wept for my beloved James.

In this land full of many bones such as the many skulls lining every memorial hall, I wrestled with questions of *why?* and *how?* Walking in the room dedicated to remembering the children at the main memorial in Kigali, I was always reminded of the importance of sharing individual stories. Large pictures of children lined the walls with a plaque underneath saying the child's name, age, what they liked to eat, what they liked to play, and how they were murdered.

In the hallway dedicated to all the genocides of the world, I noticed the patterns of cruelty and how Satan had craftily used the leaders of the world to take the focus off the value of one human life and stir up hate for an entire people group. These leaders used the same methodologies to unleash hate and cruelty, such as measuring noses or issuing identification cards that would indicate each person's tribe, religion, and physical features. They belittled people by calling them derogatory names and taught the youth to dehumanize and devalue them, leading to mass murder.

The serpent in the Genesis account who lost his position in heaven (Ezekiel 28:11-19) has hated the human race since Adam was created in the garden of Eden and given authority to rule (Gen 2:28). Jesus describes him as "a murderer from the beginning, and does not stand in the truth, because there is no truth in him" (John 8:44 NASB). That ancient serpent (Revelation 12:9) continues to resent humankind, and his aim is to make us doubt God and to kill, steal, and destroy us (John 10:10), even dividing us one against another; but God gave His beloved Son Jesus to give us life and give it abundantly (John 10:10).

Despite the invisible raging war I was becoming more aware of in my spiritual journey, I could also see life and hope springing up in the hardest places along some of the dusty, rocky roads we traveled outside the city. Meeting widows in far off villages, I was often inspired by their stories of perseverance and faith despite all they had passed through.

Our team met an older widow in Rugendabari, Mama Moses, who exemplified James's exhortation to care for widows and orphans in their distress (James 1:27). This woman, with a humble home made with sticks and mud, no running water nor electricity, had taken in two orphaned boys in her village as her own, nursing the youngest in her old age (something I didn't know was possible). When we asked what she had been praying for, she told us that she had been praying for a field to give to these boys as an inheritance. She had even picked out the field, which was situated next to the mayor, making it safer. She had mapped out how she'd use half of the field for subsistence farming to help with their food supply and the remainder to grow trees for the boys to sell for profit ten years down the road.

God used the generosity from Apple of His Eye Charity to provide the widow with the exact amount she needed to buy that field. We gathered for the transaction and signed as witnesses that the land would be inherited by these boys. I was absolutely amazed by this woman's desire to not only provide for them in the short-term, but also to ensure they had an inheritance for the future. She reminded me of the Proverbs 31 woman, who considered a field and bought it to care for her household. What a picture her life exemplified of God adopting us and giving us an inheritance in Christ!

I also was moved by the testimonies I heard from the students at the vocational center from where I worked most days. One woman in her early twenties told my colleagues and me, with tears welling up in her eyes, "I am now ready to forgive those who killed my parents."

While I saw these incredible, powerful God stories, I also saw material poverty. Daily I was confronted of how to help the poor, as people literally showed up to our gate. One day while backing out of our house with Jake and Lizzy in the back, an older woman was holding a child that appeared malnourished or extremely sick. I didn't understand Kinyarwanda, and so to help explain, she lifted up her shirt, grabbed her breasts, and shook them violently in front of us. Obviously, there was no milk, so I went to get her some milk. As we'd travel downtown, sometimes a child ran up to me and say, "Give me my money," or a child with a somber face would come begging at my car window with their mother or auntie around the corner. Diana often reminded me not to give money. With a soft and most generous heart, always giving her possessions freely, she'd constantly meet people at our gate and talk with them to discern what was the best way to handle every person.

I wrestled with all these daily decisions. I desired to follow Christ's commands but was in a state of stress, asking, *"What does God say about giving to the poor? And how should I help the poor without hurting them?"* These questions lingered as I saw the effects of charity, some of which created unhealthy dependency. I could see there was undealt with trauma that kept people from moving forward. At the same time, I saw people working hard labor and extremely long hours, waking up at 3 or 4 a.m. to work in the fields, in security or construction jobs, working six or seven days a week, in order to support their families. Every time I went to exchange money, I'd greet a man sitting by the entrance who faithfully shined shoes and did other jobs. I always admired him, working faithfully, and yet he had no legs, no wheelchair, and moved around on his hands. When exiting the exchange, another man who had only one leg, would direct traffic for me so that I could back the car out. I was always happy to pay him for his services.

As I was confronted with these realities, I felt like I was in a state of gray and usually only more questions arose. *What does God mean by healing? Is it physical? Spiritual? Both?* As I searched the Scriptures, God began to open my eyes to my own heart and my own brokenness. I started to see my own war zones, the many lies and propaganda I had been fed and believed in my own home culture, my own poverty, my own sinful reactions to pain, my own trauma I was stuck in, and the need for a deep cleaning within. I needed to go on a road to really learn about my own depravity and need for wholeness. As much as I had worked on grieving, there was far more work left to be done, for the greatest grief was not the loss of my husband, but my own sin and the destruction it had caused.

Slowly, God began to prune me, cutting into my most tender roots. Part of that deeper journey began when I met a tall Australian woman named Linda. At church one day during the time of greeting, Linda turned around to me with a friendly expression and shook my hand as she introduced herself. From there, our friendship grew.

She invited me to attend an Ellel training about healing at her house. I was quite skeptical because of all the false teaching about this topic, as I regularly heard, "Give a $100 for your miracle," on the Christian Broadcasting Network. Yet I loved my friend and wanted to learn about Jesus as Healer, and so I attended the training and was pleasantly surprised by the incredible love by the staff and volunteers and the deep theological teaching. I continued to attend trainings at her house, and our relationship grew further as she invited me for afternoon tea on many occasions while our daughters played together.

As we worshipped Jesus, prayed and dug into the Scriptures, I began to scratch the surface of the deep work of healing God wanted to do in me.

The process of healing entered every facet of my life in Rwanda. In a small group Bible study, I found myself surrounded by many medical professionals: Anita, a physical therapist, her husband Emmanuel, a neurosurgeon, two eye doctors, and an occupational therapist. A woman named Noella shared one evening that she had been widowed a couple of years earlier, when her husband had a terrible motorcycle accident.

Anita, Noella, and I started meeting earlier to intercede for the nation of Rwanda, His church, and one another; and through our times together, they were building me up and training me to be a warrior of faith. We would circle around the church praying, and then found ourselves by many hospital beds praying for the sick. We also attended Ellel trainings together, so we'd go deep, sharing the ways God was helping us to heal.

While God was nurturing me to wholeness, He continued to astonish me with His work in my children's lives, too. After about six months in Rwanda, Lizzy and Jake entered a new school called Kigali International

Community School (KICS), and it was in Lizzy's third grade classroom with Mr. Bryan that she made a decision to commit her life to the Lord. Later her friend Evey decided to be baptized on Easter Sunday, and Lizzy wanted to go the same day. I can't think of a better way to celebrate Christ's resurrection! She was surrounded by our loving church, Noella, Anita's and Linda's families, many small group members, and many of her teachers at KICS. Teachers continued to invest in her, including her learning support teacher, Mrs. Bryan, who would intentionally invest in her, meeting her each week to walk around the neighborhood.

God continued working in Jake's life, too. Jake often wrote about his dad in English assignments, sharing his deepest hurts. He vocalized it, too, standing before older orphans at the vocational center, pleading, "Don't be angry with God." He would explain how he had been angry about his father's death, but how God was healing him from his anger. While he didn't want to move to Africa, he actually fit right in, making close friendships. One family friend practically adopted him, as Jake was always at his house, attending every birthday party and wedding celebration. He ended up being a part of many family photos with them. He absolutely loved being surrounded by such big families with uncles, aunties, cousins, brothers, and sisters. As an extreme extrovert who loves to entertain a crowd, he thrived in this cultural environment where large families and frequent, unplanned visitors was the norm. He was well received and loved.

Like Jake, I think we were all thirsty for family, especially with our loss and being in a foreign land. We jumped into many English-speaking fellowships. I attended a women's Bible study fellowship, and then our family went to a church called CCR as well as another Sunday afternoon house church. I knew it was a bit over the top, but maybe I craved for answers among these fellowships or I longed for community to fill the empty space.

As our faith family grew in Rwanda, our own family also came to visit us the summer of 2015. My parents came to generously pour out love, which they did! They came with me to visit widows in their homes, visited some of the churches we partnered with, met many of our new friends like Diana, and most especially loved on the kids and me. One day when my dad took the kids swimming, he ended up teaching one of Lizzy's teachers how to swim (something many Rwandans are not taught). My dad also visited students at the vocational center and expressed his one regret was not spending more time with us, his family.

My mom also shared about her rough upbringing with students there. She made a connection between her father's experience as a soldier during the Holocaust with their experience of genocide. Like them, she was the second generation from the war. She encouraged the twenty and thirty-year-old students not to stuff down their pain as she saw her father do.

Her dad rarely spoke about his time overseas. He had bulldozed bodies after the war ended, and so when he returned to the U.S.A., he turned to alcohol to drown out his trauma. Though he had suffered post-traumatic stress disorder, he was never diagnosed or treated, and so he unintentionally passed along emotional damage to my mom. On one such occasion, when my mom flicked on the light in her parents' home, she saw a barrel pointing at her face. Her dad suspected that she was a robber. Thankfully no shot was fired.

Even though my mom had never been through war as he had, she suffered the consequences of the trauma that was swept under the rug for her generation to deal with. Forgiveness was the only way she could stand tall and express love as she was with those students at the vocational center. As she spoke to them, her radiant smile beamed love. She had always wanted to be a medical missionary in Africa, but her parents thought she was foolish to want to be a missionary. Then one day she saw blood and felt squeamish, so she knew that wasn't her path. Though her dream diminished, her desire remained. And here she was, speaking to students in Africa, just as she had spoken into students' lives as a public high school English teacher for more than thirty years. Before she left, she offered to give a hug to every student, and one-by-one, they came to receive her loving embrace.

God continued to bring more family in our lives in unique ways, too. TJ, whom I had met in Spokane at the missions conference, came to Rwanda with her new husband, along with her daughter and close friend, Sarah. We went together to a few churches to provide retreats for widows at new churches. TJ's husband was an eye doctor, so he set up an eye clinic while TJ taught about our spiritual eyes. One day while traveling to a church, we discovered that we both had a brother-in-law who had committed suicide. Though losing a husband and brother-in-law is not the way we might want to connect with someone, the experience was powerful because of *Who* had brought us through those dark valleys. We shared our testimonies in Christ at every retreat.

At one retreat, about twenty or so older ladies sat near the front, and many people were peeking through the windows without glass and entry ways without doors. The rays of the sun shone through the roof, as half of it was not yet finished. After teaching and testimonies, TJ was led to have an altar call, and a small group of people came from outside the church to give their lives to Jesus, little ones and young adults coming into God's family - His kingdom expanding before us. At another retreat, one woman's eyes opened wide as she put on reading glasses for the first time, marveling and praising God that she could now read the precious Word of God.

All of these experiences were pointing to healing. No, I didn't witness someone who was blind who could now see (although, He does do this), but I could see the healing of the heart taking place as people were seeing Jesus with new eyes, just like the new eyes He was giving me. Like that church in the process of being built, there was much work yet to be done in my own soul, too.

Another team came to visit us, our beloved church family from Spokane, WA. Jake, Lizzy and I were elated! For two weeks, they sat with us drinking Fanta with our new friends and worshipping with us at our church and home fellowship. They sat with us by the graves, too, entering their stories as they had done with us through our loss. They traveled the dusty roads with us to go to churches in far off places, singing with joy worship songs as they played their guitars in the car. Going from church to church, our pastor Galen taught ministers and pastors, while the rest of the team provided mini-vacation Bible activities and lessons for the children. Jake and Lizzy were right alongside them, wrapping their arms around the little kids who sat close by their side as they listened to hear the stories being told.

With the heart ache of having to leave family and friends behind in the States, God continuously reminded me He was right there and would

143

never leave nor forsake us (Matthew 28:20). This also meant He'd be with me as I entered the most painful places in my own heart, too.

I had been holding off going to a healing retreat, but one day I finally mustered up the courage to attend. I was a ball of stress, feeling like I was going to the dentist to get my teeth pulled. I don't know why I was afraid, but I was. On the way I even hit the curb, but somehow managed to drag myself to go. My prayer partners awaiting me at the retreat were dear friends, Leah and Catherine, who would meet me for long periods of time over the next few days, allowing the Holy Spirit to guide our time of prayer together while others interceded for us all.

As the three of us sat together, the Lord gently reminded me of ways I had rebelled against Him. I confessed, as the Lord reminded me. The Holy Spirit helped me enter tender roots of pain in my family, such as forgiving my grandfather for his treatment of my mom after WWII and the pornography my husband had entertained that had affected our marriage. The more I forgave, the more free I became. I was even led to forgive the entire porn industry, recognizing that I had become bitter towards them. It's like chains were broken off that I didn't know were there. Our times of prayer were full of mercy and love as they tenderly nurtured me to face everything God showed me, and then allowed the space and time for God to heal those areas.

During one of the quiet times while sitting alone outside with my Bible with the lush greenery and flowers around me, Jesus gave me a very special gift – the meaning of my name. I thought my name had no significance, only feeding a lie that I had no worth or value. I learned that *heather* is a flower that grows in rocky, high places and survives grazing and fires. I was reminded of how He had brought me through many fires in life. Although I thought my husband was the "survivor" because of his many battles with cancer and brave acts, I came to realize that I was a survivor, too, only because of Christ who never left my side. I left that retreat refreshed and restored.

Healing – it's not a process I often want to enter. It hurts when the alcohol is poured on a burn, but that's exactly what I needed. I needed to allow God to bind up my broken heart. Jesus came into some deep, shameful places, and by allowing Him to walk through every corner and in every hole, He tenderly surrounded me with people to come alongside me to the edge of the grave, to repent, and watch Him plant and spring life from it. The process of healing is not yet complete, but He is still at work, with the final consummation of completeness occurring when He returns again.

The Spirit of the Lord God is upon me,
Because the Lord has anointed me
To bring good news to the afflicted;
He has sent me to bind up the brokenhearted,
To proclaim liberty to captives,
And freedom to prisoners;
To proclaim the favorable year of the Lord,
(see Jesus reading in this scroll in Luke 4:18-19)

And the day of vengeance of our God;
To comfort all who mourn,
To grant those who mourn in Zion,
Giving them a garland instead of ashes,
The oil of gladness instead of mourning,
The mantle of praise instead of a spirit of fainting.
So they will be called oaks of righteousness,
The planting of the Lord, that He may be glorified.
-Isaiah 61:1-3
New American Standard Bible

~ 19 ~

HIS REDEMPTION

1-2-3! LIFT! A guide would shout as we pushed the raft high above our heads to toss on the tall stack. Carrying the weight of those rafts after the exhaustion of paddling the river with customers was never easy. After all the work was done, on both good days and bad, I could sit back in the bus and look at the river from another vantage point as we drove the mountain roads. The customers could, too, as they talked with excitement about the adventures they had with their guide. Even if their boat flipped and they were knocked up a bit by the river rocks, they could look at it and talk about what a wild adventure they shared together and survived together. Usually the rougher the trip made it all the more memorable. I was always at peace exiting the river, back on the bus, unlike how I usually felt when I dipped my feet in the water. As I sighed with the completion of another day of work, I could now rest until another day of adventure began.

December 2015 – May 2017 (Kigali, Rwanda)

As my two-year contract came to an end, I was not at peace about leaving Rwanda nor continuing on with the ministry in which I came. After much prayer and gaining wise counsel from many, I discovered another organization that was looking for help. As I sat down with their director, I learned that they were coaching and training entrepreneurs and had recently started a social-enterprise working with women in prostitution. As I shared with her my past experience working with small businesses and my vision to tell God stories, support business start-ups, and invest in their spiritual lives, she invited me to join the team.

Before long, I found myself in a completely different environment working in an office in Kigali, whereas before I commuted 45 minutes to work in an office out of the city and frequently went even further to make home visits. Instead of being the only "muzungu" on the team, I was now on an international team of multiple nationalities where everyone spoke English. For months I was going through another culture shock. I missed my former workplace, working with various teams and visiting churches in remote villages. I went from working with vocational students, many who were orphaned and widowed, to working with university students and entrepreneurs. No longer meeting with the widows was the hardest, as it's like my identity had been entangled in that word. Everywhere I went, I spoke about my widowhood to relate with the people, but now I was surrounded by people who didn't understand widowhood as I had experienced.

As I slowly stepped into their stories, though, I discovered people with similar stories, displaying the same perseverance through adversity, and I continued to be inspired. All the while, I think maybe God was working to strip me from this firm grip I had on my identity as a widow and to pull me up out of the ashes into something new.

One such woman who sprung life into my step was an intern named Rita. She was studying communications at university, and everyday I saw her, she'd sing worship songs as she skipped up the stairs to the office. I later learned that as a child, her parents left her to care for her siblings while they worked across the border in the Congo. They were in this critical situation for nearly ten years, and she explained to me that she thought she might end up being a street girl like all the others. But rather, God's plan was radically different. This slender and petite woman was ambitious, strong, and nothing could ignite the fire in her! Her dream was to be a journalist and to become an advocate for the poor.

As the social-enterprise got off the ground, I was able to take a peak into what God was doing among other women. I marveled as my teammates recollected going to the streets to pay prostitutes for one hour to talk, inviting them to come to a facility to learn and make jewelry. As the women came, I got little glimpses into their stories as I went to the training center and heard the staff reports. Many of the women came to the city for an opportunity, but due to lack of jobs and skills, had no other available options. Some had even been house workers who were raped by their employer and then cast out on the streets.

The team went to great lengths to care for them holistically, with regular counseling, a social worker, another watching their children while they worked, and daily training in a new skill. They were also earning income for the jewelry they made. However, it was evident that receiving love and trusting us would take time to build.

It was difficult to connect with them, especially without understanding Kinyarwanda and having a shared experience, but one way I identified with most of them was as a single mother. I could empathize with their desperation to pay for school supplies or seek medical attention when their kids were sick. I also grappled with their children's experiences, orphaned in a sense, and possibly feeling unwanted as different men passed by. As I came to know bits and pieces of their families' lives, I saw a greater loss was to never have experienced unconditional love.

Going to make visits, sitting with them on their mattress in those dimly lit rooms, we could see their life more clearly. With varying stories, the same thread of abuse, abandonment and shame was seen; but our team believed and hoped that a greater thread of redemption could break through the pain and callous. One woman seemed pretty rough around the edges. Sitting on her bed, I quietly prayed as Marlene spoke to her. As I quieted my soul, I saw a miner going deep in the mountain for this one rock. After going deep, deep down, he dusted off a rock which turned out to be a shimmering diamond. I shared it with Marlene for her to pass on, expressing God's great value for her and the great depths He has gone to in order to rescue and restore her to Himself. We continued to pray for her, and all the ladies, that they would believe Jesus and the great sacrifice He made to save us.

Just as God was working to redeem these women's lives, He was also redeeming mine, too, developing a self-awareness of how He formed me. My purpose and vocational calling was something I had wrestled with my entire life, but most especially after the loss of James and the many lost dreams that were buried with him, too.

In May 2016, just before my kids and I took time to travel back to the states, I had a vivid dream about James, but it was unlike any dream I had had before. In the dream I went on a wild adventure, leaving James behind at a hotel and telling him I'd return. I traveled down cobblestone roads, entering a small, brightly colored cottage house with stained glass windows, passing through parades of wild characters dressed in costumes, and even made it to a mountain full of planes to chit chat with Presidents, before going as far as the ocean shore. As I walked along the beach, I suddenly recalled that I needed to go back to James. I immediately turned around and started running to return, but the waves started crashing high and overtaking the beach. I kept going, determined to return, running past the mountain, down the cobble stone road, passing the cottage house, and climbed up the stairs to the hotel, even pushing a skateboarder out of the way who gave me trouble. But then as I entered the doors of the hotel, I remembered, *Oh, he's dead*.

That dream was a significant moment where the tides began to turn. I was finally starting to release James and to come to terms with my new reality. After four and half years of sifting through the complexity of this curse called death, I was able to grasp that he's gone. I could embrace the new beginnings, rather than trying to return to the old. James would never have taken these adventures with me, because they weren't meant for us to share. That chapter had concluded.

After six months of working at this new organization, our family went back to the states for a few months, but before landing in America, we took a short stop in Amsterdam. We walked the streets, seeing people smoke marijuana openly on the street, so I had to explain what they were smoking to Jake and Lizzy. "Um, that's not a cigarette, and those aren't coffee shops." We almost stumbled upon the "red light district" where women are provocatively standing in windows. I felt completely out of place having come from East Africa.

I decided we should attend a local church and located a Hillsong Church in the city center. On Sunday morning, we entered what appeared to be a bar or night club, and later learned they were renting it for their services. *Redemption*, I thought. Everyone was so kind, offering us cake as we came in or assisting with our coats, and then the big screen said, "Welcome Home." It was so refreshing, as it seemed every country we entered always felt at home when we were gathered with God's family.

After the service, we planned to go to the Anne Frank House, but I needed some help finding the place. I immediately was drawn to a woman with dark African-looking skin and asked her for help. She eagerly agreed and asked us to wait to get her sister. She said they used to work there and would walk us there. *No coincidence,* I thought.

During that walk, we eagerly exchanged our stories and how we ended up in Amsterdam. We learned Precious and Nicole came from some rough backgrounds. As we spoke, and seeing us shivering in the chilly, drizzly weather, they took us into a shop and offered to buy us sweatshirts. I tried to refuse, but they insisted and bought each of us a sweatshirt. Precious encouraged me to receive the blessing and allow them to shower us with love. Receiving God's love – that seemed to be the message I continued to hear the last year as I allowed God to come into some hard places and pamper me with lots of love and care.

By the time we arrived at the Anne Frank House, we didn't want to depart. We still had an hour, so they insisted once again to treat us to a true "Dutch" pancake, so off we went to a local diner. As we chatted more, Nicole shared her story of being homeless and living on couches, but how God had cared for her and moved her into the music industry to be a vessel of light. Precious was studying communications, and like me, she was hoping to write her first book. We left that diner so loved and satisfied.

That evening walking the halls of Anne Frank's house, I was bubbling from excitement of our encounter with them. I was also strolling down the lane of another genocide, entering this little girl's story of being hidden and her journalism career coming to fruition… but after her death. I remembered my grandfather and what he must have witnessed.

Before we left Amsterdam, they came to our hotel room to pray for us. At 10 p.m. at night, my daughter crawled into her bunk bed, and Jake and I bowed our heads to receive prayer. Precious was on her knees by my side, and Nicole sat next to Jake. As they prayed over each of us, the Lord convicted us both while also restoring us with Scriptures to carry us through. Specifically, I was reminded of His work to bring "beauty from ashes" in this season (Isaiah 61) and that He would show the way (Isaiah 30:21) to go in the many chapters ahead.

The next day we flew to the States and were soon back on American soil at the Hartsfield International Airport. I eagerly shared all that had happened with my mom and dad at a local restaurant, and they marveled to hear all God's work. But I hadn't shared everything, and little by little, shared some of the healing God was doing in my own heart.

Later during the summer, my mom handed me a letter from her mom, my grandmother Nony, titled "Dear daughter." This letter indicated that my grandfather Bill had gone to a brothel during the war, had fallen in love, and almost didn't return back to Nony and my mom, who was about two years old by that time. However, he did come back. He met them at the train station, meeting my mother for the first time. While Nony must have struggled to cope with this different man who came back from the war, she revealed they never discussed that letter. That was the mode of operation for the silent generation, as they called them. As I sat there with my mom, holding the letter, I was reminded of forgiving the pornographic industry, and then I could see the redemption thread in our own family's story. Maybe, just maybe, He had me working with these women in prostitution to not only help me heal but my mother, too.

Returning to Rwanda, I had a renewed sense of purpose and excitement after having been loved on by many, including Precious and Nicole, my parents, and the churches in which we visited. I continued to see God's work, especially among one of the women at the social-enterprise named Josee. As we prayed together, she stopped asking for prayer for rent money and school fees, and she began to ask for an intimate relationship with Christ. I was a bit skeptical, as often people would make a confession of faith in order to receive monetary gain, but as the weeks continued and her prayers remained, Marlene encouraged me that she was starting to have faith in Christ and was connecting to a local fellowship of believers.

While I continued to be in amazement, I began to wonder if it was time for us to leave Rwanda, praying fervently about it. I saw all these Rwandans fully alive in faith, capable, equipped and boldly sharing the gospel with their nation. For many of those whom I met, poverty was their greatest obstacle, as there was always need for rent, food, transport money, and school fees. The daily obstacles of providing for physical needs was a real challenge to survive for many. However, I could see God giving them rich faith that many in this world lacked – a spiritual poverty worse than all, lacking a relationship with their Creator.

I absolutely loved the people, didn't want to leave, but I could see my role was no longer needed. I began thinking beyond the borders and asking, *What about those who have no church, no Christian, and have yet to hear the good news?*

Early one beautiful, sunny morning, I sat on our porch reading my Bible. Every once and a while, I'd look up at the sky to watch birds soar through the air. That particular morning, as I prayed about whether or not I should leave Rwanda, I asked that if it was His will for us to leave, He might send us to people who hadn't yet heard about Jesus. Just as soon as I prayed, one of the soaring birds landed right at the corner of our white marble porch. This kite was not like a little humming bird—one had stolen a hotdog from our friend Gianni just before he had taken a bite to eat. They were like vultures! In all my days in Rwanda, I had never seen a kite on the ground, as they tended to stay high up in the towering trees. As I looked into the bird's eyes with fear, I wondered, *What in the world is he going to do?* Just as quickly as that thought passed through my mind, he nodded three times! Then he spread his wings and took off just as quickly as he had landed. In my spirit, I knew that God was confirming that it was time for us to leave our nest in Rwanda and to venture further beyond.

The kids were elated to return to America, but I told them I wasn't sure how long we'd be there, prefacing we might go to another country. They were nervous, but the excitement of returning to America for a time overturned those anxieties.

When talking with Lizzy one day, she said, "Mom, I think we are going to Asia." I about blew over, because in my spirit, I felt the same. I gathered them in the living room one evening to pray about a country and wait upon the Lord, having been encouraged by a woman with a organization that we were potentially going to join. We were on our knees, and I asked for Him to show us. I then heard *Cambodia* in my heart three times and shared it with the kids. I rose from the ground to go to the wall with our world map, not having a clue where it was. Low and behold, it was situated in Southeast Asia. Telling my pastor via email, his first response was recollecting the Khmer Rouge of the late 1970s. He thought it was interesting that it would be another country that had gone through genocide.

Only a week later I was attending our house fellowship, and somehow missed the memo that they weren't having it this particular week. Arah welcomed me in and invited me to watch a sermon online with her and her husband. We didn't know each other that well, so we began to share some of our back stories. She and her family were Filipino and had lived in many African countries. With three children, one had graduated and was at university in the states, and two of the children were going to school with Jake and Lizzy at KICS. Arah had previously worked with World Vision, but now she was a CEO of a bank in Kigali.

In the conversation, I shared about how God was stirring my heart to leave. I recollected our prayer and hearing *Cambodia*, and as I spoke, Arah's face lit up. She replied, "Heather, we used to live in Cambodia before moving here, and we have been praying for more workers to be sent there." I was shocked! We both were! She then invited our family to come for dinner so they could tell us about this country that they had grown to love.

Within a week, Jake, Lizzy and I were back at her house, learning how to make beautiful dragon style sushi with avocado, cucumber and carrots. Jake devoured as much sushi as they'd let him (it's one of his favorite dishes), and we enjoyed the other Asian dishes they prepared and sipped on tea as we learned about Cambodia, including options for the kids' schooling.

God continued to speak into me about next steps the months before our departure. As I wrapped up an Ellel 12-day discipleship school at Linda's house, I met with two people to pray in a small room while others interceded for us outside. The woman praying for me was inspired to share Jeremiah 1, and then as all of us gathered again, those interceding for us spoke the same exact verses. They also strengthened us, expressing that they were very prompted to share about taking the gospel to the nations. I left that training full of encouragement from the Lord.

Saying goodbye to Rwanda, though, did not come easy. It also came in many stages and waves, as we had to share the news gradually to allow space for closure. The hardest was leaving Dianna who had become like family, living with us for the last three years and practically helped raise Jake and Lizzy, taking them hot lunches to school when they forgot, cleaning their clothes, and making them African tea and treats to eat after school. I told her six months in advance to give her time to find a new job and to start her new season without us. As I told her the news, we both wept. It was extremely hard. Eventually she found a new job, and we hired another gentleman named Sam to come cook for us until we left.

In those final months, every morning I would open the kitchen door to hear ruckus as a mouse ran across our countertop. One day, I looked at him straight in the eyes, thinking, *I see you*! I sprinkled poison and laid traps in hopes to get rid of him. One day, I came downstairs to smell something wretched. I asked Sam what that smell might be, and he pulled back the counter tops to find that mouse dead in the corner. He grabbed it by the tail and took it to bury in the corner of our yard. *Good riddance!*

Within a week, a big mushroom started to grow out of that little mound of dirt, and a week later Sam came to ask if he might take that mushroom home to eat it. "Enjoy it!" I said. He was beaming with excitement to take it, and I marveled at the whole situation. How interesting that this mushroom would blossom from this dead mouse, and the blessing it would be to him. It had become a little reward for all his labors for removing it and burying it in our backyard.

And that story stuck with me in my departure of Rwanda. Life had sprung up, resulting in something useful and nourishing. That joy Sam had over the mushroom was something I was experiencing, too, along with the satisfaction from it. All the sadness I experienced there and with the loss of James helped me savor in a far deeper way the simplest, most profound details of life. It was the lit-up face of a little boy running after me in the slums, the intricate beauty of a flower or watching a bird soar, or the old woman's crinkled hands weaving bowls on her lap. I think our whole family had learned to appreciate and thank God for daily food, for water, and found joy dancing in the pouring rains.

Life had sprung up from the grave, resulting in something useful and nourishing.

Though foreigners, we had become comfortable and had somehow found a little nook in their society. Jake and Lizzy had formed community through their school. I didn't realize the extent of how deep those relationships had become until drawing closer to our time to leave. I was especially touched by the rich relationship my daughter shared with her teacher, and that goodbye was terribly difficult for her to face. Jake spent most of his last weeks spending the night with his friend Gianni, and I tried to make efforts to meet with individuals and create opportunities to say goodbyes, knowing I might not see people again.

I also had to wrap up work, and during our final weeks, a whirlwind of events were taking place. One of the highlights was that Josee gave her life to Christ, and Marlene and I had the great pleasure to go to the river to watch her being baptized.

Simultaneously, my coworker, a counselor by profession, was going through turmoil as her husband fought for his life in the ICU. After months in a coma, he died, leaving behind his wife and family. After the funeral, Marlene and I went to her house to visit, and as we sat in her house with her daughter sitting nearby, she was sullen, yet full. She knew that her husband was with Jesus in heaven, and though she was strong and full as I had been when my husband died, I knew there would be a long journey ahead for her and her family. I gave her a handkerchief that had been given to me after James died, which had been sprinkled with hand-written Scriptures. It had become tattered, stained and worn over the years as I had passed through my own sorrows.

The day before I departed Rwanda, this widow came to where I was staying to say goodbye. I was deeply touched that she had made the time and effort to come see me before my departure. She handed me a wooden bird and a card that explained that this bird was to represent peace. I spilled over in tears as I read her note, for I had arrived in Rwanda in the warm embrace of widows who called me *Uwamhaoro* and was now being sent off with peace by another.

As we exited this beautiful garden tucked in East Africa, we left with shalom.

And the Lord God planted a garden toward the east, in Eden; and there He placed the man whom He had formed. And out of the ground the Lord God caused to grow every tree that is pleasing to the sight and good for food; the tree of life also in the midst of the garden, and the tree of the knowledge of good and evil. Now a

river flowed out of Eden to water the garden; and from
there it divided and became four rivers.
-Genesis 2:8–10
New American Standard Bible

And he showed me a river of the water of life, clear
as crystal, coming from the throne of God and of the
Lamb, in the middle of its street. And on either side
of the river was the tree of life, bearing twelve kinds of
fruit, yielding its fruit every month; and the leaves of
the tree were for the healing of the nations. And there
shall no longer be any curse; and the throne of God and
of the Lamb shall be in it, and His bondservants shall
serve Him; and they shall see His face, and His name
shall be on their foreheads.
-Revelation 22:1–4
New American Standard Bible

～ 20 ～

EPILOGUE

WHILE LIVING IN the "garden of Africa," the master Gardener met me personally as He meandered through the garden of my heart, cutting out the twigs and giving me water to refresh my weary soul. In this season of my life, I encountered Jesus radically as He took me deeper into His story, entering the searing grief, the poverty, the sickness, the bloody cross, and the life from death. I was often reminded of the Garden of Eden, where trees blossom and rivers flow. It's a place mixed with both creation and destruction, life and death, triumph and tragedy. They were cast out, not to eat from the tree of life forever and remain broken, but as a good and faithful gardener, God has patiently been working out His plan (2 Peter 3:9), calling people to repent and obey, pruning and cutting His people to bear more fruit (John 15:1-2), until it's time for harvest.

February 2018 (Spokane, WA to Phnom Penh & Kep, Cambodia)

My adventures with the Lord continued as He guided my heart through the grief of losing again while also preparing me to enter another nation. He allowed time for me to breathe, to reflect, and to discover Him in a long season of waiting and continued pruning as I went into theological training in Spokane.

In February 2018, our family landed in Phnom Penh for a short two-week visit. Gathered with a group of families, huddled on the floor at the White Elephant Resort, a tall man stood up and shared about the Mekong

River, explaining how it merges with the Tonle Sap, causing a reversal flow of water each year. Like these merging rivers, he said, we too were merging together in this particular place and in this season of time. He asked us to reflect on the rivers of our lives, about the history that had brought us to this intersection at the Mekong and Tonle Sap. As each family recounted their stories, I saw us yet again intertwining in a community who had been through similar intense rapids – of cancer, of leaving nations, of loss. Within a year, many of those families would be redirected like the Tonle Sap, leaving Cambodia to go to other nations or returning to their passport country.

Later that week, Jake, Lizzy and I stood on the rim of another massive hole at Shalom Valley, a new Christian adventure camp that was on the verge of construction. Craig, the founder, huddled all of us there that day around the bomb crater and asked, "What do you do in the absence of shalom?" The question was piercing, as I looked at the emptiness of this hole left by the US Strategic Air Command during the Vietnam War. I had pondered and questioned it for so many years. *What do you do when everything falls apart – when war erupts and casualties are massive? Who will fill that empty space?*

As we continued to walk and pray around the property, Lizzy took notice of a little green plant sprouting from the red dirt and zoomed in to take a picture. It's one of those plants that when you touch it, even softly, it opens up. Like that plant, I've come to realize to move on and move beyond, reconciliation with God is really the only way to healing and wholeness. If I fill that space with anything else, I will remain with an emptiness that will never be satisfied, storing up bitterness, weeds and death. But if I allow Him to touch me, just as many came to Jesus to be touched to receive healing, He will make me new and bring life from disaster.

I'm thankful Jesus led me to the rapids of the Ocoee to meet James and far beyond those rapids to all these places and peoples in order to encounter Him. Oh, the depth and riches of knowing Him! So I'll keep paddling and crossing rivers, to know Him, the power of His resurrection and the fellowship of His sufferings (Philippians 3:10), until the day He calls me home.

But whatever things were gain to me, those things I have counted as loss for the sake of Christ. More than that, I count all things to be loss in view of the surpassing value of knowing Christ Jesus my Lord, for whom I have suffered the loss of all things, and count them but rubbish so that I may gain Christ, and may be found in Him, not having a righteousness of my own derived from the Law, but that which is through faith in Christ, the righteousness which comes from God on the basis of faith, that I may know Him and the power of His resurrection and the fellowship of His sufferings, being conformed to His death; in order that I may attain to the resurrection from the dead. Not that I have already obtained it or have already become perfect, but I press on so that I may lay hold of that for which also I was laid hold of by Christ Jesus. Brethren, I do not regard myself as having laid hold of it yet; but one thing I do: forgetting what lies behind and reaching forward to what lies ahead, I press on toward the goal for the prize of the upward call of God in Christ Jesus.
-Philippians 3:7-14
New American Standard Bible

CPSIA information can be obtained
at www.ICGtesting.com
Printed in the USA
BVHW071330220720
584347BV00002B/119